# AN AVESTA GRAMMAR IN COMPARISON W
# AVESTAN ALPHABET AND ITS TRANSCRIP
# VALENTINE WILLIAMS JACKSON

## Publisher's Note

The book descriptions we ask book-sellers to display prominently warn that this is an historic book with numerous typos or missing text; it is not indexed or illustrated.

The book was created using optical character recognition software. The software is 99 percent accurate if the book is in good condition. However, we do understand that even one percent can be an annoying number of typos! And sometimes all or part of a page may be missing from our copy of the book. Or the paper may be so discolored from age that it is difficult to read. We apologize and gratefully acknowledge Google's assistance.

After we re-typeset and design a book, the page numbers change so the old index and table of contents no longer work. Therefore, we often remove them; otherwise, please ignore them.

Our books sell so few copies that you would have to pay hundreds of dollars to cover the cost of our proof reading and fixing the typos, missing text and index. Instead we let most customers download a free copy of the original typo-free scanned book. Simply enter the barcode number from the back cover of the paperback in the Free Book form at www.RareBooksClub.com. You may also qualify for a free trial membership in our book club to download up to four books for free. Simply enter the barcode number from the back cover onto the membership form on our home page. The book club entitles you to select from more than a million books at no additional charge. Simply enter the title or subject onto the search form to find the books.

If you have any questions, could you please be so kind as to consult our Frequently Asked Questions page at www. RareBooksClub.com/faqs.cfm? You are also welcome to contact us there. General Books LLC™, Memphis, USA, 2012.

AVESTA GRAMMAR IN COMPARISON WITH SANSKRIT AND THE AVESTAN ALPHABET AND ITS TRANSCRIPTION AMS PRESS NEW YORK FK

AN

AVESTA GRAMMAR

IN COMPARISON WITH SANSKRIT

BY

A. V. WILLIAMS JACKSON

OF COLUMBIA COLLEGE, NEW YORK CITY

Part I

Phonology, Inflection, Word-formation

WITH AN INTRODUCTION ON THE AVESTA

Jackson, Abraham Valentine Williams, 1862-1937.

An Avesta grammar in comparison with Sanskrit together with The Avestan alphabet and its transcription.

Reprint of 2 works published by W. Kohlhammer, Stuttgart:

pt. 1 of An Avesta grammar in comparison with Sanskrit originally published in 1892, and The Avestan alphabet and its transcription in 1890.

Pt. 2 of the first work never published. Cf. BM.

Bibliography: p.

Includes index.

1. Avesta language—Grammar. 2. Avesta language-Transliteration. I. Jackson, Abraham Valentine Williams, 1862-1937. The Avestan alphabet and its transcription. 1975. II. Title.

PK6103.J23 1975 491'.52'5 77-149387

ISBN 0-404-09010-9

Reprinted from the editions of 1892 and 1890, Stuttgart

First AMS edition published in 1975

Manufactured in the United States of America

AMS PRESS INC.

NEW YORK, N. Y. 10003

Inscribed to

Professor K. F. Geldner with gratitude and regard.

## Preface.

The present Grammar is a work of no pretensions; it is offered as a small contribution toward advancing the Avesta cause. It is written in part fulfilment of a design formed when I first began to study the Avesta and became deeply interested in the true value and importance of that monument of antiquity.

The end for which the book is intended would perhaps have been better accomplished, however, if the work had been a mere grammatical sketch. This was my first design; and it may at another time be carried out. But as the work grew under my hands, it seemed desirable to enlarge it somewhat further, and to embody additional material which for reference might be serviceable to the general philologist, not to the specialist alone. The linguist may thus find in it useful matter and fresh illustrations, especially in the new readings from Geldner's edition of the Avesta texts.

No attempt, on the other hand, has been made to secure absolute completeness. Numerous minor points have been purposely omitted. These may perhaps later be taken up in a more extended work including also the Old Persian by the side of the Avesta and the Sanskrit. Little of importance, however, it is believed, has been overlooked. A fairly symmetrical development has been aimed at, although at times certain less familiar points have received fuller illustration than those that are well-known. This was intentional. They are chiefly matters that had not as yet been sufficiently emphasized elsewhere, or points which are peculiarly individual to the Avesta. They will easily be recognized.

The method of treatment is based throughout on the Sanskrit grammar; a knowledge of Sanskrit is presupposed. At every step, therefore, references have been made to Whitney's *Sanskrit Grammar* 2 ed. 1889; and it is a pleasure here to express thanks to the author of that work for the abundant suggestions received from it.

In the Grammar it might have been easier and more practical in many respects to use the Avesta type itself instead of employing a transcription. On the whole, however, it seemed best under the circumstances to transliterate. For general reference at present this method appears more convenient, and is useful in showing grammatical formations. The original type, it is expected, will be employed, as hinted above, in a little book *Avesta for Beginners,* planned for a date not far distant.

In regard to the transcription here adopted, my views have already been given in *The Avestan Alphabet and its Transcription,* Stuttgart, 1890. The phonetic and palaeographic character of each of the Avestan letters is there discussed. Reasons are likewise presented for transliterating Av. (, j by the 'turned' *3, 3,* so familiar in phonetic works. The composite *d (ag)* for *r"* ((-»") is also there explained (p. 13). The choice of the old Germanic characters *li, j, p, d* for the spirants , *6,* , and for the nasal *v* (1), as well as the method of transliterating (1-)--") by *h' (h--v)* is defended (pp. 14, 21). The 'tag' (t) appearing in the letters */, Ij, q, h., q* is an attempt at systematically representing the 'derivation stroke' *j* by which many of the letters palaeographically are formed. Thus, *r* H, 10 (p, w *(r,* w i w.f, o 99 etc.— the dotted line denoting the 'derivation stroke'. See *Av. Alphabet* pp. 16—17. The same 'tag' appears in the transcription f S (c + u) by *$ (e--s).* See *Av. Alphabet* p. 20. In the case of ro / (beside *$),* the 'subscript' tag is merely turned in the opposite direction so as to correspond with the hooked part (9) of the letter. The threefold differentiation *s, $, /* for o, gj. To, 's not necessary, how-

ever, except in transliterating a text for purely scientific purposes. In practise, *s* may everywhere be written. A 'substitute alphabet' to be used in popular articles is offered in the same monograph p. 28. I wish again to repeat my thanks to the authorities there quoted *(Av. Alphabet* p. 7) who so kindly aided me with advice and suggestions in regard to the transcription adopted.

In reference to the transliteration of Sanskrit, the familiar system (cf. Whitney, *Skt. Gram.* § 5) is followed; but be it observed that for comparison with the Avesta it seems preferable to transcribe the palatal sibilant by *s* (Whitney f), the palatal nasal by « (Whitney «), the guttural nasal by *v* (Whitney n).

A word may now be added in regard to my manifold indebtedness in the present book. The general grammatical works from the early contribution of Haug *Essays,* 1862), through Hovelacque *Grammaire,* 1868) down to the present date have been on my table. Justi's *Handbuch der Zendsprache* (1864) was of course consulted continually. Constant reference has been made also to Bartholomae's *Altiranische Dialekte* (1883) and to his other admirable grammatical contributions. Spiegel's *Vergl. Gram, der altfran. Sprachen* (1882) was often opened, and will be specially acknowledged with others under the Syntax (Part II). C. de Harlez' *Manuel de E Avesta* (1882), Darmesteter's *Etudes Iraniennes* (1883), W. Geiger's *Handbuch der Azvestasprache* (1879) furnished more than one good suggestion, for which I am much indebted.

Acknowledgment is also due to some special contributions on grammatical subjects. In the Phonology, selections were made from the rich material collected by Hubschmann in *KuhtCs Zeitschrift* xxiv. p. 323 seq. (1878). My indebtedness to that well-known standard work Brugmann's *Grundriss der vergl. Gram. (= Elements of Compar. Grammar of the Indg. Languages,* English translation by Wright, Conway, Rouse, 1886 seq.) may be noticed from the citations below. Under Declension, frequent reference was made to Horn's

*Nominalflexion im Avesta* (1885) and Lanman's *Noun-Inflection in the Veda* (1880).. Under Verbal Inflection, in addition to Bartholomae's contributions below cited, acknowledgments are due to other authors to be mentioned in connection with Syntax (Part II). Caland's *Pronomina im Avesta* (1891) unfortunately came too late for the Inflections, but is cited under the Syntax of the Pronouns. I also regret that the work of Kavasji Edalji Kanga, *A Practical Gram, of the Av. Language* (1891) was not received in time. My indebtedness to Whitney's *Skt. Gram.* is noticed above. For grammatical training in Sanskrit, moreover, I shall always thank my teachers in America and Germany— Professors Perry, Hopkins, and Pischel.

To my honored instructor and friend, Professor K. F. Geldner of Berlin, I owe, as I have owed, a lasting debt of gratitude. The book was begun when *1* was a student under his guidance; since I returned to America it has progressed with the aid of his constant encouragement, suggestion, and advice. He has been kind enough, moreover, not only to read the manuscript, as it was sent to Stuttgart, but also to look through the proof-sheets before they came back to me in America. The work I may call a trifling expression of the inspiration he gave me as a student. Let what is good in it count as his; the faults are my own.

It is a pleasure to add my cordial thanks to the publisher, Herrn W. Kohlhammer, for the characteristic interest which, with his usual enterprise, he has taken in the work. Special praise is due to his compositor, Herrn A. Sauberlich, whose accuracy is in general so unfailing that I fear I must say that the misprints which may have escaped notice are probably due to original slips of the author's pen, and not to inaccuracies on the part of the type-setter— a thing which cannot always be said. I should like also to express to Messrs. Ginn & Co., of Boston and New York, my appreciation of their willing co-operation in advancing the Iranian as well as other branches of the Oriental field in America.

The present part of the Grammar

(Part I) is confined to the Introduction, Phonology, and Morphology. The prefatory sketch of the Avesta and the Religion of Zoroaster may perhaps prove not without use. The second volume (Part II), a sketch of the Syntax, with a chapter also on Metre, is already half in print, and is shortly to appear. The numbering of sections in the second part will be continued from the present part; the two may therefore be bound together as a single volume if preferred.

With these words and with the suggestion to the student to observe the Hints for using the Grammar, given below, and to consult the Index, the book is offered to the favor of Oriental scholars. Any corrections, suggestions, or criticisms, which may be sent to me, will be cordially appreciated and gladly acknowledged.

October 1891.

A. V. Williams Jackson

Columbia College

New York City. INTRODUCTION.

Avesta: The Sacred Books of the Parsis.1

The Avesta as a Sacred Book.

§ 1. The Avesta, or Zend-Avesta, as it is more familiarly, though less accurately called, is the name under which, as a designation, we comprise the bible and prayer-book of the Zoroastrian religion. The Avesta forms to day the Sacred Books of the Parsis or Fire-Worshippers, as they are often termed, a small community living now in India, or still scattered here and there in Persia. The original home of these worshippers and of their holy scriptures was ancient Iran, and the faith they profess was that founded centuries ago by Zoroaster (Zarathushtra), one of the great religious teachers of the East.

§ 2. The Avesta is, therefore, an important work, preserving as it does, the doctrines of this ancient belief and the customs of the earliest days of Persia. It represents the oldest faith of Iran, as the Vedas do of India. The oldest parts date back to a period of time nearly as remote as the Rig-Veda, though its youngest parts are much later. The religion which the Avesta presents was once one of the greatest; it has, more-over, left ineffaceable traces upon the history of the world. Flourishing more than a thousand years before the Christian era, it became the religion of the great Achsemenian kings, Cyrus, Darius, and Xerxes, but its power was weakened by the conquest of Alexander, and many of its sacred books were lost. It revived again during the first centuries of our own era, but was finally broken by the Mohammedans in their victorious invasion. Most of the Zoroastrian worshippers were then compelled through persecution to accept the religion of the Koran; many, however, fled to India for refuge, and took with them what was left of their sacred writ 1 This sketch, with additions and some alterations, is reprinted from my article AVESTA, simultaneously appearing in the *Internationat Cyclopaedia;* for which courtesy I am indebted to the kindness of the Editor, my friend, Professor H. T. Peck, and that of the Publishers, Messrs. IJodd, Mead & Co., New York.

ings. A few of the faithful remained behind in Persia, and, though persecuted, they continued to practise their religion, It is these two scanty peoples, perhaps 80,000 souls in India, and 10,000 in Persia, that have preserved to us the Avesta in the form in which we now have it.

§ 3. The designation *Avesta,* for the scriptures, is adopted from the term *Avistiik,* regularly employed in the Pahlavi of the Sassassian time. But it is quite uncertain what the exact meaning and derivation of this word may be. Possibly Phl. *Avistak,* like the' Skt. *Veda,* may signify 'wisdom, knowledge, the book of knowledge'. Perhaps, however, it means rather 'the original text, the scripture, the law'. The designation 'ZendAvesta', though introduced by Anquetil du Perron, as described below, is not an accurate title. It arose by mistake from the inversion of the oftrecurring Pahlavi phrase, *Avistak va Zand* 'Avesta and Zend', or 'the Law and Commentary'. The term *Zand* in Pahlavi (cf. Av. *aza'titi-),* as the Parsi priests now rightly comprehend it, properly denotes 'understanding, explanation', and refers to the later version and commentary of the Avesta texts, the paraphrase which is written in the Pahlavi language. The proper designation for the scriptures, therefore, is *Avesta;* the term *Zend* (see below) should be understood as the Pahlavi version and commentary.

Allusions to the Avesta; its Discovery and History of Research.

§ 4. Of the religion, manners, and customs of ancient Persia, which the Avesta preserves to us, we had but meagre knowledge until about a century ago. What we did know up to that time was gathered from the more or less scattered and unsatisfactory references of the classic Greek and Latin, from some allusions in Oriental writers, or from the later Persian epic literature. To direct sources, however, we could not then turn. Allusions to the religion of the Magi, the faith of the Avesta, are indeed to be found in the Bible. The wise men from the East who came to worship our Saviour, the babe in Bethlehem, were Magi. Centuries before that date, however, it was Cyrus, a follower of the faith of Zoroaster, whom God called his anointed and his shepherd (Isaiah 45. 1,13; 44.281, 2 Chron. 36.22,23; Ezra 1. 1 —11) and who gave orders that the Jews be returned to Jerusalem from captivity in Babylon. Darius, moreover (Ezra 5.13 —17; 6.1 —16), the worshipper of Ormazd, favored the rebuilding of the temple at Jerusalem as decreed by Cyrus. Allusions to the ancient faith of the Persians are perhaps contained in Ezek. 8.16; Is. 45.7,12. See also Apocryphal New Test., The Infancy, 3.1 —10.

§ 5. The classical references of Greek and Roman writers to the teachings of Zoroaster, which we can now study in the Avesta itself, may be said to begin with the account of the Persians given by Herodotus (B.C. 450) in his History 1.131 —141. To this account may be added references and allusions, though often preserved only in fragments, by various other writers, including Plutarch 'On Isis and Osiris', and Pliny, down to Agathias (A. D. 500).

§ 6. After the Mohammedan conquest

of Persia, we have an allusion by the Arabic writer, Masudi (A. D. 940), who tells of the *Avesta* of Zeradusht (Zoroaster), and its commentary called *Zend,* together with a *Pazend* explanation. The *Abasia* (Avesta) is also mentioned several times by Al-BTruni (about A. D. 1000). The later Mohammedan writer, Shahrastani (A. D. 11501, sketches in outline the creed of the Magi of his day. An interesting reference is found in the Syriac-Arabic Lexicon of *Rar-Bahlftl* (A. D. 963) to an *Avastak,* a book of Zardusht (Zoroaster), as composed in seven tongues, Syriac, Persian, Aramsean, Segestanian, Marvian, Greek, and Hebrew. In an earlier Syriac MS. Commentary on the New Testament (A. D. 852) by Tsho"diid, Bishop of Hadatha, near Mosul, mention is made of the Abhastft as having been written by Zardusht in twelve different languages. These latter allusions, though late, are all important, as showing the continuity, during ages, of the tradition of such a work as the Avesta, which contains the teachings of Zoroaster, the prophet of Iran. All these allusions, however, it must be remembered, are by foreigners. No direct Iranian sources had been accessible.

§ 7. From this time, moreover, till about the 17th century we find there was little inquiry into the sacred books of the Persians. One of the first series of investigations into the Greek and Roman sources seems then to have been undertaken by a European, Barnabe Brisson, *De Persarum Principatu* (Paris 1590). The Italian, English, and French travelers in the Orient next added some information as to the religion and customs of the Persians. Among them may be mentioned the works of Pietro della Valle (1620), Henry Lord (1630), Mandelso (1658), Tavemier (1678), Chardin (1721), I)u Chinon. Most important, however, was the work of the distinguished Oxford scholar, Thomas Hyde (1700). It was written in Latin, and entitled *Historia Retigionis veterum Persarum.* Hyde resorted chiefly to the later Parsi sources; the original texts he could not use, although an Avesta MS. of the Yasna seems to have been brought to

Canterbury as early as 1633. Hyde earnestly appealed to scholars, however, to procure MSS. of the sacred books of the Parsis, and aroused much interest in the subject. In 1723 a copy of the Vendidad Sadah was procured by an Englishman, George Boucher, from the Parsis in Surat and was deposited as a curiosity in the Bodleian Library at Oxford.

§ 8. No one, however, could read these texts of the Avesta. To a young Frenchman, Anquetil du Perron, belongs the honor of first deciphering them. The history of his labors is interesting and instructive. Happening, in 1754, to see some tracings made from the Oxford MS., and sent to Paris as a specimen, du Perron at once conceived the spirited idea of going to Persia, or India, and obtaining from the priests themselves the knowledge of their sacred books. Though fired with zeal and enthusiasm, he had no means to carry out his plan. He seized the idea of enlisting as a soldier in the troops that were to start for India, and in November, 1754, behind the martial drum and fife this.youthful scholar marched out of Paris. The French Government, however, recognizing at once his noble purpose, gave him his discharge from the army and presented him his passage to India. After countless difficulties he reached Surat, and there after innumerable discouragements, and in spite of almost insurmountable obstacles, he succeeded in winning the confidence and favor of the priests, with whom he was able to communicate after he had learned the modern Persiari. He gradually induced the priests to impart to htm the language of their sacred works, to let him take some of the manuscripts, and even to initiate him into some of the rites and ceremonies of their religion. He stayed among the people for seven years, and then in 1761, he started for his home in Europe. He stopped at Oxford before going directly to Paris, and compared his MSS. with the one in the Bodleian Library, in order to be assured that he had not been imposed upon. The next ten years were devoted to work upon his MSS. and upon a translation, and

in 1771, seventeen years from the time he had first marched out of Paris, he gave forth to the world the results of his untiring labors. This was the first translation of the Avesta, or, as he called it, Zend-Avesta *(Ouvrage de Zoroastre,* 3 vols., Paris 1771), a picture of the religion and manners contained in the sacred book of the Zoroastrians.

§ 9. The ardent enthusiasm which hailed this discovery and opening to the world of a literature, religion, and philosophy of ancient times was unfortunately soon dampened. Some scholars, like Kant, were disappointed in not finding the philosophical or religious ideas they had hoped to find; while others missed the high literary value they had looked for. They little considered how inaccurate, of necessity, such a first translation must be. Though Anquetil du Perron had indeed learned the language from the priests, still, people did not know that the priestly tradition itself had lost much during the ages of persecution or oblivion into which the religion had fallen. They did not sufficiently take into account that Anquetil was learning one foreign tongue, the Avesta, through another, the modern Persian; nor did they know how little accurate and scientific training du Perron had had. A discussion as to the authenticity of the work arose. It was suggested that the so-called Zend-Avesta was not the genuine work of Zoroaster, but was a forgery. Foremost among the detractors, it is to be regretted, was the distinguished Orientalist, Sir William Joncs. He claimed, in a letter published in French (1771), that Anquetil had been duped, that the Parsis had palmed off upon him a conglomeration of worthless fabrications and absurdities. In England, Sir William Jones was supported by Richardson and Sir John Chardin; in Germany, by Meiners. In France the genuineness of the book was universally accepted, and in one famous German scholar, Kleuker, it found an ardent supporter. He translated Anquetil's work into German (1776, Riga), for the use of his countrymen, especially the theologians, and he supported the genuineness of those scriptures by classical allusions to the Magi. For nearly fifty years, however, the battle as to authenticity, still raged. Anquetil's translation, as acquired from the priests, was supposed to be a true standard to judge the Avesta by, and from which to draw arguments; little or no work, unfortunately, was done on the texts themselves. The opinion, however, that the books were a forgery was gradually beginning to grow somewhat less.

§ 10. It was the advance in the study of Sanskrit that finally won the victory for the advocates of the authenticity of the Sacred Books. About 1825, more than fifty years after the appearance of du Perron's translation, the Avesta texts themselves began to be studied by Sanskrit scholars. The close affinity between the two languages had already been noticed by different scholars; but in 1826, the more exact relation between the Sanskrit and the Avesta was shown by the Danish philologian, Rask, who had travelled in Persia and India, and who had brought back with him to the Copenhagen library many valuable MSS. of the Avesta and of the Pahlavi books. Rask, in a little work on the age and authenticity of the Zend-Language (1826), proved the antiquity of the language, showed it to be distinct from Sanskrit, though closely allied to it, and made some investigation into the alphabet of the texts. About the same time the Avesta was taken up by the French Sanskrit scholar, Eugene Burnouf. Knowing the relation between Sanskrit and Avestan, and taking up the reading of the texts scientifically, he at once found, through his knowledge of Sanskrit, philological inaccuracies in Anquetil's translation. Anquetil, he saw, must often have misinterpreted his teachers; the tradition itself must often necessarily have been defective. Instead of this untrustworthy French rendering, Burnouf turned to an older Skt. translation of a part of the Avesta. This was made in the 15th century by the Parsi Naryosangh, and was based on the Pahlavi version. By means of this Skt. rendering, and by applying his philologial learning, he was able to restore sense to many passages where Anquetil had often made

nonsense, and he was thus able to throw a flood of light upon many an obscure point. The employment of Skt., instead of depending upon the priestly traditions and interpretations, was a new step; it introduced a new method. The new discovery and gain of vantage ground practically settled the discussion as to authenticity. The testimony, moreover, of the ancient Persian inscriptions deciphered about this time by Grotefend (1802), Burnouf, Lassen, and by Sir Henry Rawlinson, showed still more, by their contents and language so closely allied to the Avesta, that this work must be genuine. The question was settled. The foundation laid by Burnouf was built upon by such scholars as Bopp, Haug, Windischmann, Westergaard, Roth, Spiegel —the two latter happily still living—and to day by Bartholomae, Darmesteter, de Marlez, Hubschmann, Justi, Mills, and especially Geldner, including some hardly less known names, Parsis among them. These scholars, using partly the Sanskrit key for the interpretation and meaning of words, and partly the Parsi tradition contained in the Pahlavi translation, have now been able to give us a clear idea of the Avesta and its contents as far as the books have come down to us, and we are enabled to see the true importance of these ancient scriptures. Upon minor points of interpretation, of course, there are and there always will be individual differences of opinion. We are now prepared to take up the general division and contents of the Avesta, and to speak of its Tahlavi version.

Contents, Arrangement, Extent, and Character.

§ 11. The Avesta, as we now have it, is but a remnant of a once great literature. It has come down in a more or less fragmentary condition; not even a single manuscript contains all the texts that we now have; whatever we possess has been collected together from various codices. All that survives is commonly classed under the following divisions or books: 1. *Yasna,* including the *Gathas* 2. *Vtspercd* 3. *Yashts* 4. Minor texts, as *Xyaishes, Gahs* etc. 5. *Vendidad* 6. Fragments, from *H*

&*dhokht Xask* etc.

§ 12. In the first five divisions two groups are recognized. The first group (i) comprises the Vendidad, Vispered, and Yasna; these as used in the service of worship are traditionally classed together for liturgical purposes and form the Avesta proper. In the manuscripts, moreover, these three books themselves appear in two different forms, according as they are accompanied, or not, by a Pahlavi version. If the books are kept separate as three divisions, each part is usually accompanied by a rendering in Pahlavi. On the contrary, however, these three books are not usually recited each as a separate whole, but with the chapters of one book mingled with another for liturgical purposes, on this account the MSS. often present them in their intermingled form, portions of one inserted with the other, and arranged exactly in the order in which they are to be used in the service. In this latter case the Pahlavi translation is omitted, and the collection is called the Vendidad Sadah or 'Vendidad pure' i.e. text without commentary, (ii) The second group comprising the minor prayers and the Yashts which the MSS. often include with these, is called the *Khordah Avesta* or 'small Avesta'. Of the greater part of the latter there is no Pahlavi rendering. The contents and character of the several divisions, including the fragments, may now be taken up more in detail.

§ 13. (1) The *Vnsua,* 'sacrifice, worship', is the chief liturgical work of the sacred canon. It consists principally of ascriptions of praise and prayer, and in it are inserted the *GatMs,* or 'hymns', verses from the sermons of Zoroaster, which are the oldest and most sacred part of the Avesta. The Yasna (Skt. *yajna*) comprises 72 chapters, called *Hd, Hiiti.* These are the texts recited by the priests at the ritual ceremony of the Yasna *(Izashne).* The book falls into three nearly equal divisions. (a) The first part (chap. 1 — 27) begins with an invocation of the god, Ormazd, and the other divinities of the religion; it gives texts for the consecration of the holy water, *zaotkra,* and the *baresma,* or bundle of sacred twigs, for the preparation and dedication of the Haoma, *haoma,* the juice of a certain plant — the Indian Soma — which was drunk by the priests as a sacred rite, and for the offering of blessed cakes, as well as meat-offering, which likewise were partaken of by the priests. Interspersed through this portion, however, are a few chapters that deal only indirectly with the ritual; these are Ys. 12, the later Zoroastrian creed, and Ys. 19—21, catechetical portions.— (b)Then follow the Gathas lit. 'songs', 'psalms' (chap. 28—53), metrical selections or verses containing the teachings, exhortations, and revelations of Zoroaster. The prophet exhorts men to eschew evil and choose the good, the kingdom of light rather than that of darkness. These Gathas are written in meter, and their language is more archaic and somewhat different from that used elsewhere in the Avesta. The Gathas, strictly speaking, are five in number; they are arranged according to meters, and are named after the opening words, Ahunavaiti, Ushtavaiti etc. The Gathas comprise 17 hymns (Ys. 28—34; 43—46; 47—50; 51, 53), and, like the Psalms, they must later have been chanted during the service. They seem originally to have been the texts or metrical headings from which Zoroaster, like the later Buddha, preached. In their midst (chap. 35—42) is inserted the so-called Vasna of the Seven Chapters *(Yasna HaptanghSiti).* This is written in prose, and consists of a number of prayers and ascriptions of praise to Ahura Mazda, or Ormazd, to the archangels, the souls of the righteous, the fire, the waters, and the earth. Though next in antiquity to the Gathas, and in archaic language, the Haptanghaiti represents a somewhat later and more developed form of the religion, than that which in the Gathas proper was just beginning. Under the Gathas also are included three or four specially sacred verses or formulas. These are the Ahuna Vairya or Honovar (Ys. 27.13), Ashem Vohu (Ys. 27.14), Airyama Ishyo (Ys. 54.1) and also the Yenghe Ilatam (Ys. 4.26), so called from their first words, like the Pater Noster, Gloria Patri, etc., to which in a measure they

answer.—(c) The third part (chap. 52, 55—72) or the 'latter Yasna' *(aparo yasno)* consists chiefly of praises and offerings of thanksgiving to different divinities.

§ 14. (2! The *Vispered* (Av. *vispi ratavo)* consists of additions to portions of the Yasna which it resembles in language and in form. It comprises 24 chapters (called *Karde),* and it is about a seventh as long as the Yasna. In the ritual the chapters of the Yispered are inserted among those of the Yasna. It contains invocations and offerings of homage to 'all the lords' *(vispi ratavo).* Hence the name Yispered.

§ 15. (3) The *Yashts* (Av. *yesti* 'worship by praise') consist of 21 hymns of praise and adorations of the divinities or angels, *Yazatas (Izads),* of the religion. The chief Yashts are those in praise of ArdviSura, the goddess of waters (Yt. 5), the star Tishtrya (Yt. 8), the angel Mithra, or divinity of truth (Yt. 10), the Fravashis, or departed souls of the righteous (Yt. 13), the genius of victory, Verethraghna (Yt. 14), and of the Kingly Glory (Yt. 19). The Yashts are written mainly in meter, they have poetic merit, and contain much mythological and historical matter that may be illustrated by Firdausi's later Persian epic, the Shah Xamah.

§ 16. (4) The minor texts, *XySishes, oShs, Strozahs, Afringans,* consist of brief prayers, praises, or blessings to be recited daily or on special occasions.

§17. (5) The *Iemiidadi* or 'law against the daevas, or demons' *(vtdacva data),* is a priestly code in 22 chapters (called *Fargard),* corresponding to the Pentateuch in our Bible. Its parts vary greatly in time and in style of composition. Much of it must be late. The first chapter Farg. 1) is a sort of an Avestan Genesis, a dualistic account of creation. Chap. 2 sketches the legend of Yima, the golden age, and the coming of a destructive winter, an Iranian flood. Chap. 3 teaches, 'among other things, the blessings of agriculture; Chap. 4 contains legal matter — breaches of contract, assaults, punishments; Chap. 5—12 relate mainly to the impurity from the dead; Chap. 13—15 deal chiefly

with the treatment of the dog; Chap. 16—17, and partly 18, are devoted to purification from several sorts of uncleanness. In Chap. 19 is found the temptation of Zoroaster, and the revelation; Chap. 20-»-22 are chiefly of medical character. In the ritual, the chapters of the Vendidad are inserted among the Gathas.

§ 18. (6) Besides the above books there are a number of fragments, one or two among them from the *Iladhokht A'ask.* There are also quotations or passages from missing Nasks, likewise glosses and glossaries. Here belong pieces from the *Nirangistin, Aogemadalca, ZandPahlavi Glossary,* and some other fragments. These are all written in the Avesta language, and are parts of a once great literature. Under the Zoroastrian religious literature, moreover, though not written in Avesta, must also be included the works in Pahlavi, many of which are translations from the Avesta, or contain old matter from the original scriptures.

§ 19. From the above contents, it will be seen that our present Avesta is rather a Prayer-Book than a Bible. The Vendidad, Vispered, and Yasna were gathered together by the priests for liturgical purposes. It was the duty of the priests to recite the whole of these sacred writings every day, in order to preserve their own purity, and be able to perform the rites of purification, or give remission of sins to others. The solemn recital of the Vendidad, Vispered, and Yasna at the sacrifice might be compared with our church worship. The selections from the Vendidad would correspond to the Pentateuch when read; the preparation, consecration, and presentation of the holy water, the Haoma-juice, and the meat-offering, described in the Yasna and Vispered would answer to our communion service; the metrical parts of the Yasna would be hymns; the intoning of the Gathas would somewhat resemble the lesson and the Gospel, or even the sermon. In the Khordah Avesta, the great Yashts might perhaps be comparable to some of the more epic parts of our Bible; but as they are devoted each to some divinity and preserve much of the old mythology, they really have hardly a parallel, even in the apocryphal books.

§ 20. Such, in brief outline, is the contents of the books known to-day as the Avesta; but, as implied above, this is but a remnant of a literature once vastly greater in extent. This we can judge both from internal and from historical evidence. The character of the work itself in its present form, sufficiently shows that it is a compilation from various sources. This is further supported by the authority of history, if the Parsi tradition, going back to the time of the Sassanidae, be trustworthy. I'liny *(Hist. Nat.* 30.1,2) tells of 2,000,000 verses composed by Zoroaster. The Arab historian, Tabari, describes the writings of Zoroaster as committed to 12,000 cowhides (parchments); other Arabic references by Masudi, and Syriac allusions to an Avesta, which must have been extensive, have been noted above § 6. The Parsi tradition on the subject is contained in the Rivayats, and in a Pahlavi book, the Dinkard. The Dinkard (Bk. 3) describes two complete copies of the Avesta. These each comprised 21 Nasks, or Nosks (books). The one deposited in the archives at Persepolis, as the Arda Viraf says, perished in the flames when Alexander burned the palace in his invasion of Iran. The other copy, it is implied, was in some way destroyed by the Greeks. From that time the scriptures, like the religion under the Groeco-Parthian sway, lived on, partly in scattered writings and partly in the memories of the priests, for nearly 500 years.

§ 21. The first attempt again to collect these writings seems to have been begun under the reign of the last Arsacida?, just preceding the Sassanian dynasty. Pahlavi tradition preserved in a proclamation of King Khusro Anoshirvan (6th cent. A. D.), says it was under King Valkhash, probably Vologoses I., the contemporary of Nero, that the collection was begun of the sacred writings as far as they had escaped the ravages of Alexander, or were preserved by oral tradition. Valkhash was among the last of the Arsacida.'. The Sassanian dy-

nasty (A. D. 226) next came to the throne. This house were genuine Zoroastrians and warm upholders of the faith, and they brought back the old religion and raised it to a height it had hardly attained even in its palmiest days. The first Sassanian monarchs, Artakhshir Papak&n (Ardeshir Babagan, A. D. 226—240) and his son Shahpuhar I. (A. D. 240—270), eagerly continued the gathering of the religious writings, and the Avesta again became the sacred book of Iran. Under Shahpuhar II. (A. D. 309—380) the final revision of the Avesta texts was made by Atur-pat Maraspend, and then the king proclaimed these as canonical, and fixed the number of Nasks or books.

§ 22. Of these Nasks, 21 were counted, and a description of them, as noted, is found in the Rivayats, and in the Dinkard; each received a name corresponding to one of the twenty-one words in the Ahuna-Vairya (Honovar), the most sacred prayer of the Parsis. Each of these Nasks contained both Avesta and Zend, i. e. original scripture and commentary. This tradition is too important to be idly rejected. Its contents give an idea of what may have been the original extent and scope of the Avesta. The subjects said to have been treated in the 21 Nasks may practically be described in brief, as follows: Nask 1 (twenty-two sections), on virtue and piety; 2 (likewise twenty-two sections), religious observance; 3 (twentyone sections), the Mazdayasnian religion and its teachings; 4 (thirty-two sections), this world and the next, the resurrection and the judgment; 5 (thirty-five sections), astronomy; 6 (twenty-two sections), ritual performances and the merit accruing; 7 (fifty sections before Alexander, thirteen then remaining), chiefly political and social in its nature; 8 (sixty sections before Alexander, twelve after remaining), legal; 9 (sixty sections before Alexander, fifteen later preserved), religion and its practical relations to man; 10 (sixty sections before Alexander, only ten afterwards surviving), king Gushtasp and his reign, Zoroaster's influence; 11 (twenty-two sections originally, six preserved after

Alexander), religion and its practical relations to man; 12 (twenty-two sections), physical truths and spiritual regeneration; 13 (sixty sections), virtuous actions, and a sketch of Zoroaster's infancy; 14 (seventeen sections), on Ormazd and the Archangels; 15 (fiftyfour sections), justice in business and in weights and measures, the path of righteousness; 16 (sixty-five sections), on next-of-kin marriage, a tenet of the faith; 17 (sixty-four sections), future punishments, astrology; 18 (fiftytwo sections), justice in exercising authority, on the resurrection, and on the annihilation of evil; 19, the Videvdad, or Vendidad (twenty-two sections, still remaining), on pollution and its purification; 20 (thirty sections), on goodness; 21 (thirty-three sections), praise of Ormazd and the Archangels.

§ 23. During the five centuries after the ravages of Alexander much, doubtless, had been lost, much forgotten. The Parsi tradition itself acknowledges this when it says above, for example, that the seventh Nask consisted originally of 50 sections, but only 13 remained 'after the accursed Iskander (Alexander)'. So says the Dinkard and so the Rivayats. Like statements of loss are made of the eighth, ninth, tenth, eleventh Nasks. The loss in the five centuries from the invasion of Alexander, however, till the time of the Sassanian dynasty, was but small in comparison with the decay that overtook the scriptures from the Sassanian times till our day. The Mohammedan invasion in the seventh century of our era, and the inroad made by the Koran proved far more destructive. The persecuted people lost or neglected many portions of their sacred scriptures. Of the twenty-one Nasks that were recognized in Sassanian times as surviving from the original Avesta, only one single Nask, the nineteenth—the Vendidad — has come down to us in its full form. Even this shows evidence of having been patched up and pieced together. We can furthermore probably identify parts of our present Yasna and Vispered with the Staot Yasht *(staota yesuya)* or Yasht *(yesnya),* as it is also called. The two fragments Yt. 21 and

22 (as printed in Westergaard's edition) and Yt. 11, in its first form, are recognized in the MSS. as taken from the 20th, or Hadbokht Nask. The Xirangistan, a l'ahlavi work, contains extensive Avestan quotations, which are believed to have been taken from the Husparam, or 17th Nask. Numerous quotations in Pahlavi works contain translations from old Avestan passages. The Pahlavi work, ShSyastla-Shayast, quotes briefly from no less than thirteen of the lost Xasks; the Bundahish and other Pahlavi works give translations of selections, the original Avesta text of which is lost. Grouping together all the Avesta texts, we may roughly calculate that about two-thirds of the total scriptures have disappeared since Sassanian times.

§ 24. The present form of the Avesta belongs to the Sassanian period. Internal evidence shows that it is made up of parts most varied in age and character. This bears witness to the statement that during that period the texts, as far as they had survived the ravages of Alexander, and defied the corrupting influence of time, were gathered together, compiled, and edited. According to the record of Khusro Anoshirvan (A. 1). 531—579), referred to above, King Valkhash, the first compiler of the Avesta, ordered that all the writings which might have survived should be searched for, and that all the priests who preserved the traditions orally should contribute their share toward restoring the original Avesta. The texts as collected were re-edited under successive Sassanian rulers, until, under Shahpuhar II. (A. IX 309—379) the final redaction was made by his prime minister, Aturpat Maraspend. It is manifest that the editors used the old texts as far as possible; sometimes they patched up defective parts by inserting other texts; occasionally they may have added or composed passages to join these, or to complete some missing portion. The character of the texts, when critically studied, shows that some such method must have been adopted.

§ 25. Parts of the Avesta, therefore, may differ considerably from each other in regard to age. In determining this the text criticism by means of metrical restoration is most instructive. Almost all the oldest portions of the texts are found to be metrical; the later, or inserted portions, are as a rule, but not always, written in prose. The grammatical test also is useful; the youngest portions generally show a decay of clear grammatical knowledge. The metrical Gathas in this respect are wonderfully pure. They are, of course, in their form the oldest portion of the text, dating from Zoroaster himself. The longer Yashts and metrical portions of the Yasna contain much that is very old and derived doubtless from the ancient faith of Iran; but in their form and in general composition, they are probably some centuries later than the Gathas. The Vendidad is in this regard most incongruous. Some parts of it are doubtless of great antiquity, though corrupted in form; other parts, like younger portions also of the Yashts, may be quite late. The same is true of formulaic passages throughout the whole of the Avesta, and some of the ceremonial or ritual selections in the Vispered and Nyaishes, etc. ' Roughly speaking, the chronological order of the texts would be somewhat as follows: i. Gathas (Ys. 28—53) and the sacred formulas Ys. 27.13,14, Ys. 54, including also ii. Yasna Haptanghaiti (Ys. 35—42) and some other compositions, like Ys. 12, 58, 4.26, in the Gatha dialect. iii. The metrical Yasna and Yashts, as Ys. 9, 10, 11, 57, 62, 65; Vt. 5, 8, 9, 10, 13, 14, 15, 17, 19; portions of Vd. 2, 3, 4, 5, 18, 19, and scattered verses in the Vispered, Nyaishes, Afringans, etc. iv. The remaining prose portions of the Avesta.

In the latter case it is generally, but not always, easy to discover by the style and language, where old material failed and the hand of the redactor came in with stupid or prosaic additions.

§ 26. Considerable portions, therefore, of our present Avesta, especially the Gathas, we may regard as coming directly from Zoroaster himself; still, additions from time to time must have been made to the sacred canon from his day on till the invasion of Alexander. The so-called copy of the Zoroastrian Bible which it is claimed was destroyed by that invader, doubtless contained much that was not directly from the founder of the faith, but was composed by his disciples and later followers. The Parsis, however, generally regard the whole work as coming directly from Zoroaster; this is a claim that the Avesta itself hardly makes. The Gathas, however, undoubtedly came directly from the prophet; the Avesta itself always speaks of them as 'holy' and especially calls them the 'five Gathas of Zoroaster'. We may fairly regard many other portions of the Avesta as direct elaborations of the great teacher's doctrines, just as the Evangelists have elaborated for us portions of the teachings of our Lord.

§ 27. In regard to the locality in which we are to seek the source of the Avesta and the cradle of the religion, opinions have been divided. Some scholars would place it in the West, in Media; the majority, however, prefer to look to the Kast of Iran, to Bactria. Both views probably have right on their side, for perhaps we shall not be amiss in regarding the Avesta as coming partly from the Kast, and partly from the West. The scene of most of it doubtless does belong in the East; it was there that Zoroaster preached; but the sacred literature that grew up about the Gathas made its way, along with the religion to the West, toward Media and Persia. Undoubtedly some texts, therefore, may well have been composed also in Media. The question is connected also with that of Zoroaster's home which may originally have been in the West. On the native place of Zoroaster, see Jackson in *Amer. Or. Society's Journat,* May 1891 pp. 222 seq. The language itself of the texts, as used in the church, became a religious language, precisely, as did Latin, and therefore was not confined to any place or time. We may regard the Avesta as having been worked upon from Zoroaster's day down to the time of the Sassanian redaction.

Religion of the Avesta.

§ 28. The religion contained in the Avesta is best called Zoroastrianism, a name that gives due honor to its founder and which is thus parallel with Christianity, Buddhism, Mohammedanism. Other designations are sometimes employed. It has often been termed Mazdaism, from its supreme god; or again Magism, from the Magi priests; sometimes we hear it styled Fire-Worship, or even Dualism, from certain of its characteristic features. The designation Parsiism, from the name of its modern followers, is occasionally applied.

§ 29. Beyond our own Bible, the sacred books perhaps of hardly any religion contain so clear a grasp of the ideas of right and wrong, or present so pure, so exalted a view of the coming of a Saviour, a resurrection and judgment, the future rewards and punishments for the immortal soul, and of the life eternal, as does the Avesta, the book of the scriptures of ancient Iran.

§ 30. In Zoroastrianism, however, as in other religions, we recognize a development. In the older stage of the Gathas, we have the faith in its purity as taught by Zoroaster (Zarathushtra) himself, more than a thousand years perhaps before our Lord. But later, and even before the invasion of Alexander had weakened the power of the religion, we find changes creeping in. There was a tendency, for example, to restore many of the elements of the primitive faith of Iran, which Zoroaster had thrown into the background. Traces of the different stages are plainly to be recognized in the Avesta.

§ 31. The most striking feature of Zoroaster's faith, as taught in the Gathas, is the doctrine of Dualism. There are two principles, the good and the evil, which pervade the world. All nature is divided between them. These principles are primeval. Good and evil have existed from the beginning of the world. Ahura Mazda, the Lord of Wisdom (the later Persian Ormazd) is Zoroaster's god; Angra Mainyu, or the Spiritual Enemy (the later Persian Ahriman) is the devil. The evil spirit is also called Druj 'Deceit, Satan'. The good spirit and the evil are in eternal conflict. The good, Zoroaster teaches, however, will ultimately triumph. Man, a free agent, will bring the victory by choosing right and increasing the power of good. Evil shall be banished from the world. This will be the coming of the 'kingdom' or 'the good kingdom' — *vohu fy$apra*—as it is called. To the right choice Zoroaster exhorts his people. The question whence Zoroaster derived his idea of dualism, and how far he was a reformer, will not here be entered into.

§ 32. According to the prophet's teaching, Ahura Mazda, the god of good, is not without the aid of ministering angels. These are called Amesha Spentas, 'Immortal Holy Ones', the later Persian A mshaspands. They correspond in a measure to our idea of Archangels. They are six in number and constitute, with Ahura Mazda, the heavenly host. Their names are personifications of abstractions or virtues, Righteousness, Goodness, or the like. The seven-fold group, or celestial council, is as follows.

Ahura Mazda aided by
Vohu Manah
Asha Vahishta
Khshathra Vairya
Spenta Armaiti
Haurvatat
AincreUit
also
Sraosha.

These abstractions or personifications may be noticed more in detail.

§ 33-Vohu Manah (lit. 'good mind', Plutarch e5voio) is the personification of Ahura Mazda's good spirit working in man and uniting him with God. In the later development of the religion, this divinity was specialized into the good mind or kindliness that is shown toward cattle. He thus became the guardian genius of the flocks.

§ 34. Asha Vahishta (lit.'best righteousness, Plutarch dXfjSeta) is the next divinity in the celestial group and is the personification of right (Skt. *ftd)*, the divine order that pervades the world. In the heavenly court Asha stands almost in the relation of prime minister to Ormazd. To live 'according to Asha' (Right, or the Law of Righteousness e. g. Ys. 31.2) is a frequent phrase in the Avesta. The attribute *Ashavan* is the regular designation of 'the righteous', as opposed to *Dregvant* 'the wicked', or one that belongs to Satan or the Druj. In later times Asha Vahishta came to preside as guardian genius over the fire, a symbol of perfect purity.

§ 35. Khshathra Vairya or Vohu Khshathra (lit. 'the wishedfor kingdom, the good kingdom', Plutarch suvoi!a) is the personification of Ahura Mazda's good rule, might, majesty, dominion, and power, the Kingdom which Zoroaster hopes to see come on earth. The establishment of this kingdom is to be the annihilation of evil. In later times, Khshathra Vairya, as a divinity, came to preside over metals. The symbolic connection may have been suggested by the fact that the coming of the Kingdom (khshathra) was presumed to be accompanied by a flood of molten metal, the fire that should punish and purge the wicked, and which should purify the world. The metals thus became emblematic of Khshathra.

§ 36. Spent a Armaiti (lit. 'holy harmony, humility', Plutarch 009100) is the harmony, peace, and concord that should rule among men. She is represented as a female divinity; the earth is in her special charge. She plays an important part at the resurrection. The earth is to give up its dead.

§ 37. Haurvatat (Plutarch Tcxootoj) literally means 'wholeness, completeness, the saving health, the perfection', toward which all should strive, in short 'Salvation', with which word it is etymologically cognate. This divinity is always mentioned in connection with Ameretat. In the later religion, Haurvatat came to preside as guardian angel over the healthgiving w a t e r s.

§ 38. Ameretat literally means 'immortality', and is always joined with Haurvatat. In later Zoroastrianism, Ameretat presides over the trees. The pair of Haurvatat and Ameretat together seem to symbolize the waters of health and the tree of life.

§ 39. To the number of the celestial council also is to be added the divinity Sraosha (lit. 'obedience'). This genius completes the mystic number seven when Ahura Mazda is excepted from the list (cf. also Ys. 57.12). Sraosha is the angel of religious obedience, the priest god, the personification of the divine service that protects man from evil.

§ 40. Beside the above divinities in the Gathas, mention is also made of Geush T ash an, the creator of the cow, and Geush Urvan, the personified soul of the kine. We sometimes also find S p e n t a Mainyu, the Holy Spirit of Ormazd, the will of God, represented practically as a distinct personage. Lastly, the Fire, A t a r, is personified in the Gathas as one of God's ministering servants, and is a sacred emblem of the faith.

§ 41. Such is the heavenly hierarchy, and such the faith of Ormazd in which Zarathushtra exhorts the people to believe. The faithful are called Ashavans 'righteous', or later more often Mazdayasnians i. e. 'worshippers of Mazda'. This is the true religion in contradistinction to the false. The false religion is the worship of the Daevas 'demons' (Av. *daeva* opposed to Skt. *diva* 'god'). The Daeva-worshippers are misguided and live in error. They are the wicked Dregvants-(lit. 'belonging to the Druj, Satan'), 'the children of the wicked one' (St. Matt. xiii. 38—43). The two religions themselves are a part of the dualism.

§ 42. In juxtaposition to Ahura Mazda, Zoroaster sets the fiend Druj 'Deceit, Satan' or Angra Mainyu (Ys. 45. 2). The spirit of evil in coexistent with Ormazd I Ys. 30.3), but is less clearly pictured in the Gathas. In later times, to carry out the symmetry of dualism, Angra Mainyu is accompanied by a number of Arch-Fiends, in opposition to the Archangels of Ormazd. The number of the infernal group is not sharply deftned, but the chief members are

Angra Mainyu aided by
Aka Manah
Indta
Saurva
Taro-maiti
Tattru
Zairica
also
Aeshma.

Each is the opponent of a heavenly rival. Aka Manah or 'Evil Mind' is the antagonist of Yohu Manah; Taro-maiti, the demon of 'Presumption', is the opponent of Armaiti or humility; Aeshma, 'Fury, Wrath', the foe of Sraosha or holy obedience. The antagonism in the case of the others is less marked, and the connection somewhat more mechanical. ij 43. In the ftnal struggle between the two bands, the powers of light and the powers of darkness, the good eventually shall triumph. That was an ethical idea which Zoroaster inculcated. But the warfare that rages in the world between the two empires and betw een the true religion and the false, the belief in Mazda and the Daeva-worship, pervades also the soul of man and leaves the way uncertain. Yet on his choice the ultimate triumph of right or of w rong depends. Each evil deed which man commits, increases the power of evil (e.g. Ys. 31. 15); each good decd he does, brings nearer the kingdom of good. As Ahura Mazda's creature, man should choose the right. Zoroaster's mission, as shown in the Gathas (e. g. Ys. 31.2 et al.), is to guide man's choice. A summary of the prophet's moral and ethical teachings may best be given in the triad, so familiar later, 'good thoughts, good words, good deeds'. This forms the pith of the whole teaching. Purity alike of body and soul, and the choice of the good Mazda-religion rather than the wicked Daeva-worship, are inculcated. Zoroaster enjoins also the care of useful animals, especially the cow, and commends the good deeds of husbandry. He is the teacher of a higher and nobler civilization, as may be judged from the Avesta creed Ys. 12.1 seq.

§ 44. Man's actions, according to Zoroaster, are all recorded in Ormazd's sight as in a life-book (e. g. Ys. 31. 13,14, Ys. 32.6). By his own actions man shall be judged, and rewarded or punished. The doctrine of a future life, the coming of the Kingdom, the end of the world, forms a striking feature in the teachings of the Avesta. This is the tone that Zoroaster himself constantly strikes in the Gathfis. This very doctrine, and a belief also in a resurrection

of the body characterises the entire Persian faith. The resurrection is to be followed by a general judgment when evil shall be destroyed from the world. This general division and new dispensation is called the Vidaiti *(vi--da* 'dis-pose').

§ 45. The views in regard to a future life, though incomplete in the Gathas, are carried out in the Younger Avesta, and are fully given in the Pahlavi books. That the belief in a resurrection and a life hereafter was common among the Persians, some centuries before our Saviour, we have evidence in the early Greek writers, such as Theopompus, Herodotus, etc. The belief in an immediate judgment of the soul after death, the weighing in the balance, the leading of the soul across the Cinvat Bridge and through the mansions of paradise to bliss, or through the grades of hell to torment, or again in special cases to an intermediate state to await the final judgment—are all to be recognized in the Zoroastrian books and have their prototypes in the Gathiis.

§ 46. In the Yasna of the Seven Chapters, though not much later than the Gathas, we find in some respects a slight descent from the lofty level on which the religion had been placed by its founder. There is a tendency to revive ancient ideas and forms from the old worship, in which nature had played a prominent part. The elements, earth, air, fire, and water, receive adoration,- the Fravashis, or guardian angels of the righteous, are worshipped and praised together with Ahura Mazda and the Amesha Spentas. The deity Haoma, the divinity of the plant which produced the intoxicating Soma drink, again finds place in the religious rites.

§ 47. In the Younger Avesta, especially in the Yashts, we find still further restorations or innovations. The gods of the ancient mythology, like Mithra, Verethraghna, once more appear in honor by the side of the supreme deity; the divinities of the stars, moon, and sun have their share of pious worship. In the later parts of the Yasna, the sacrifice is developed into a somewhat elaborate ritual. The Zoroaster presented in certain portions of the Vendidad, moreover, is evidently no longer a living, moving personage as in the G&thas; he has become a shadowy figure, around whom time has thrown the aureola of the sprint. These passages differ widely from the old hymns; they show unmistakeable signs of lateness. They present a religion codified in the hands of the priests; superstitious beliefs and practices have found their way into the faith; intricate purifications in particular are enjoined to remove or to avoid the impurity arising from contact with the dead. The spirit of the Gathas is gone. It is only here and there that passages in late texts are old and have the genuine Zoroastrian ring. They must not be overlooked. In general, a distinction must be drawn between what is old and what is young. We must recall, as above (§ 27), that the Avesta was probably worked upon from Zoroaster's own day down to the time of the Sassanian redaction.

The Pahlavi Version of the Avesta.

§ 48. To the period of the Sassanian editing of the texts belongs the Pahlavi translation and interpretation of the Avesta. At the date when the texts were compiled and edited (§ 21), the general knowledge of the Avesta and the understanding of the sacred texts was far from perfect. The preparation of a translation or version became necessary. Accordingly, the great body of the texts was rendered into Pahlavi, the language used in Persia at the time of the Arsacidae and Sassanidse. The Pahlavi version and interpretation of the entire Yasna, Vispered, and Vendidad, with some portions of the other texts, has been preserved. We have not as yet a thorough enough understanding of this version, as the Pahlavi question is still a vexed one; but as our knowledge of this translation increases, we see more and more its importance. Owing to a somewhat imperfect knowledge of the Avesta texts at the time when the version was made, and owing to the unskilfull and peculiar manner in which the Pahlavi translation is made, this version abounds in numerous errors and inaccuracies. Its renderings, however, are often of the greatest value in interpreting allusions, particu-

larly also in giving hints for the meanings of obscure words, and in such matters it is many times our best and only guide. When more fully understood and properly used in connection with the 'comparative method', referring to the Sanskrit in interpreting the sacred texts, the 'traditional method' or native explanation is destined to win great results. The 'traditional' and the 'comparative' methods must go hand in hand.

Manuscripts of the Avesta.

§ 49. The manuscripts of the Avesta are quite numerous. Some of our specimens were copied down over five hundred years ago. They are written on parchment. The oldest was copied about the middle of the 13th century. From that date onward we have a considerable number of codices still extant. They come to us from India and from Yezd and Kirman in Persia. A number of the manuscripts are deposited in the libraries at Copenhagen, Oxford, London, Paris, Munich. The Parsi priests, especially the Dasturs, Dr. Jamaspji Minocheherji and also Peshotanji Behramji, have shown princely generosity in aiding Western scholars in editing texts by putting valuable MSS. in their possession. It is thus that the new edition of the Avesta texts by Professor Geldner of Berlin, is able to be presented in so critical a manner. No codex is complete in containing all the texts (§ 11). The different MSS. themselves, moreover, show certain variations in reading; but these chiefly affect the form and construction of single words, rather than entire passages and the sense. As a rule, the older the MS. is, the better is its grammar; and the later, the more faulty. Xotable exceptions, however, must be made, especially in favor of some later MSS. from Persia.

Importance of the Avesta.

§ 50. The importance of the Avesta, as stated above (§ 2), lies not alone in the field of philology, ethnology and early literature, but especially also is it of importance from the standpoint of comparative religion. Resemblances to Christianity in its teachings become significant when we consider the close contact between the Jews and the Per-

sians during the Babylonian captivity. These are beginning more and more to attract the attention of students of the Bible.

Language of the Avesta.

Grammatical Summary.

§ 51. The language in which the Avesta is written belongs to the Iranian branch of the Indo-Germanic tongues. With the Ancient Persian of the inscriptions it makes up the Old Iranian division. The later Iranian languages, New Persian, Kurdish, Afghan, Ossetish, Baluchi, Ghalcha, and some minor modern dialects, complete the younger division. The intervening Pahlavi and Pazand, or Parsi, do not quite complete the link between the divisions. The extent of its relationship with the Armenian is not yet defincd with sufficient exactness. On the positive kinship between the language of the Avesta and Sanskrit, see below!; 55.

§ 52. The language in which the Avesta is written may best be termed *Avesta* or *Avestan*. The designation *Avesta* for the language, as well as the book, is in keeping with the Pahlavi *AvistSk*, which is used both of the tongue and of the scriptures. The term *Avestan*, both for the language and as an adjective, is preferred by some scholars, in order to distinguish the speech from the work itself. This is sometimes found very convenient. The term *Zend* for the language, as noted above (§ 3), is a misnomer. The designation Old Bactrian, occasionally used for the tongue, has little to recommend it.

§ 53. The alphabet in which the Avesta is written is far younger than the language it presents. The characters are derived from the Sassanian Pahlavi, which was used to write down the oral tradition when the texts were collected and edited under the dynasty of the Sassanidae. The writing is read from right to left. What the original Avestan script was we do not know.

§ 54. Two dialects may be recognized in the Avesta: one the 'Gatha dialect' or the language of the oldest parts, the Gathas, or metrical sermons of Zoroaster; the other 'Younger Avesta' or the 'classical dialect'. This latter is the language of the great body of the Avesta. The Gatha dialect is more archaic, standing in the relation of the Vedic to the classical Sanskrit, or the Homeric Greek to the Attic. Possibly the Gatha language may owe some of its peculiarities noticed below, also to an original difference of locality. The Gatha dialect was the speech of Zoroaster and his followers. Its grammatical structure is remarkably pure. The younger Avesta, but only in its late compositions, owing to linguistic decay, shows many corruptions and confusions in its inflections. All that is old or is written in meter, however, is correct and accurate. Inaccuracies that have there crept in, we must generally attribute to the carelessness of the scribes. In its forms, as a rule, the Avesta is extremely antique; it stands in general on the same plane as the Vedic Sanskrit,. and occasionally, though not often, it even shows more ancient forms.

§ 55. The language of the Avesta is most closely allied to the Sanskrit, though individually quite distinct from the latter. Together they may be classed as making up an Indo-Iranian group. Almost any Sanskrit word may be changed at once into its Avestan equivalent, or vice versa, merely by applying certain phonetic laws. As example may be taken the metrical stanza Yt. 10.6 in the Avesta: *tint amavatitim yazatim surim damohu ssviStsm miprim yazai zaoprabyo—*

'Mithra that strong might)' angel, most beneficent to all creatures, I will worship with libations'—becomes when rendered word for word in Sanskrit: *tam &mavantam yajatdm suram dhamasu sdvisfham mitram yajSi hotrSbhyalf.*

§ 56. In its phonology the Avesta agrees with the Sanskrit in its vowels in general, but the Avesta shows a greater variety in using *e*-and f-sounds instead of *a*. Final vowels, except *o*, are shortened as a rule. The Skt. diphthong *l* appears in Av. as *al, di, e* (final). Thus Av. *vaenoipe* 'they two are seen'-Skt. *vin-l-te*. Skt. *ri* appears as Av. *ao, iu, ii* (final), thus Av. *aojii* 'strength' = Skt. *ojo, ojas;* A v. *l/ratiuS* 'of wisdom' =

Skt. *krdtos*. A striking peculiarity in Av. , moreover, is the introduction of epenthetic vowels and help sounds, giving rise to improper diphthongs, Av. *bava'ti* 'he becomes' = Skt. *bhdvati;* Av. *ha"rva-*'whole' = Skt. *sdrva-;* Av. *va/fdra-*'word' = Skt. *vaktra-;* Av. *lwar'-*'sun' = Skt. *svar.* The Skt. voiceless stops *k, t, p* generally become spirants *li, p, f* in Av. before consonants. Thus, Av. *apra-*'rule, kingdom' = Skt. *ksatrd-;* Av. *fra* 'forth' = Skt. *pra.* The original voiced aspirates *gh, dh, bh,* become in Av. simply voiced stops *g, d, b.* They are so preserved in the old Gatha dialect, the younger dialect commonly resolves them again before consonants and between vowels into voiced spirants. Thus, GAV. *add,* YAV. *ada* 'then' = Skt. *ddha.* Similarly spirantized in YAV. the voiced stops YAV. *ujra-,* GAV. *tigra-*'mighty' = Skt. *ugrd-.* The sibilant *s,* when initial in Skt., becomes Av. *h,* as in Greek. Thus, Av. *hapta* 'seven' = Skt. *saptd.* When internal, Skt. *s* may also appear as *vh.* Thus, Av. *vavhana-*'vesture' = Skt. *vdsana-.* Final *-as* of Skt. appears regularly as *-o.* Thus Av. *aspu* horse' = Skt. *divas.* $ 57. The Gatha dialect regularly lengthens all final vowels. It frequently inserts the anaptyctic vowels: GAV. *frti,* YAV. *frd* — Skt. *pra.* Original *ns* appears in GAV. as *tig.* Thus GAV. *dacvstig* (acc. pl.), YAV. *daevqn* 'demons' = Skt. *devdn;* GAV. *mstighSi* 'I shall think' = Skt. *mqsSi.*

§58. In inflection the Avesta shows nearly the richness of the Vedic Sanskrit. There are three genders, masculine, neuter, feminine; likewise three numbers, singular, dual, plural. The dual is not extensively used. There are eight well-developed cases of the 11 o u n and the a djective; the normal endings are: Singular. Nom. -*s;* Acc. -*im;* Instr. -*a;* Dat. -*I;* Abl. -*a(;* Gen. -*d (-as);* Loc. -*i;* Voc. —. Dual. Nom., Acc., Voc. -*a;* Instr., Dat., Abl. -*byd;* Gen. Loc. -*o,-yd.* Plural. Nom., Voc. -*d (-as),-a;* Acc. -*o (-as,-ns),-a;* Instr. -*biS;* Dat. -*byo (-byas);* Gen. -*am;* Loc. -*su,-hu,-Iva.* The classes of declension agree exactly with the Sanskrit; the method of forming comparison of adjectives likewise corresponds. The numerals answer to Skt.

forms, except Av. *aeva'onc',* opposed to Skt. *eka-,* Av. *baevar-*'10,000', but Skt. *ayuta.* The Av. pronouns closely resemble the Skt., but show also individual peculiarities. Noteworthy is the remote demonstrative Av. *ava, hau* 'that, yonder', contrasted with Skt. *amu, asau.* The verbal system in Av. and in Skt. are in general identical. The roots are chiefly monosyllabic and are subject to the same modifications as in Skt. In voice, mode, and tense, and in their conjugation-system the two languages quite agree. The endings show equal antiquity with the Sanskrit. The primary active endings in Av. are: Sing. 1, -*mi,* 2, -*hi,* 3, -*ti;* Dual. 1, -*vahi,* 3, -*to,-po;* Plur. 1, -*mahi,* 2, -*pa,* 3, -*titi.* The other endings also are parallel with the Sanskrit.

§ 59. The Av. possesses like facility with the Sanskrit in forming words by means of prefixes, and by adding suffixes of primary and secondary derivation. The same classes of compounds may be recognized in both tongues. The rules of external Sandhi, or joining together of words in a sentence, so universal in Skt., are almost wanting in Avesta. The Avesta separates each word by a dot. The vowels are fully expressed as in Greek etc., by individual letters. No diacritical points or accents are written in the texts. The meters in which the Gathas are composed have analogies in the Veda. Almost all the metrical parts of the younger Avesta are in eight-syllable lines. The syntax, however, differs from the Sanskrit in certain points, and shows some marked individualities, especially in the later portions.

Ys. 45.1 translated.

Now shall I preach, and do you give ear and hear,

Ye who hither press from near and from afar,

Therefore lay ye all these things to heart as clear

Nor let the wicked teacher your second life destroy—

The perverted sinner your tongues with his false faith.

Ys. 45.2 translated.

Now shall I preach of the world's Two primal Spirits The Holier One of which did thus address the Evil: 'Neither do our minds, our teachings, nor our concepts, Nor our beliefs, nor words, nor do our deeds in sooth, Nor yet our consciences, nor souls agree in aught.' TRANSCRIPTION OF A VEST AN ALPHABET.

(Compared with Justi, *Handbuch tier Zendsprache)* 1 Forms in parentheses () show where Justi has been deviated from. ! The signs /, » need only be employed for purely scientific purposes; the letters *y, v* for both initial and internal ro 0 », answer fully for practical purposes. 8 The differentiation /, / need only be made in scientific articles. The single sign / is ordinarily quite sufficient for the three-O, g, TO. Suggestions.

The following hints may be helpful to the student in using the Grammar. The chief points on which stress should be laid, and which it will be sufficient for the beginner to acquire, are: 1. In the Preface, the remarks on Transcription, pp. vi—vii.
2. In the Introduction, the sketch of the language of the Avesta, pp. xxx—xxxi-ii. 3. Throughout the Grammar, the large print alone need be studied. Every thing marked 'GAV.' (Gatha Avesta), and all that is in small type, may be practically disregarded. 4. Under Phonology, only the sections (§§) referred to in the Resume pp. 60—61. 5. Under the Declension of Nouns and Adjectives, the following sections should suffice: §§ 236, 243, 251, 262, 279, 291, 300, 322, 339, 362, 363. 6. Under Numerals, note merely the Cardinals § 366. 7. Under Pronouns, compare the Av. and Skt. forms in the case of §§ 386, 390, 399, 409, 417, 422, 432. No attempt need be made to commit the paradigms to memory. 8. Under Verbs, the following sections relating to the Present-System are important: §§ 448, 466,469,470,478—481,483—488. The remaining conjugations, and the Perfect, Aorist, Future, etc., may be learned as needed. 9. The rest of the book may be overlooked by the beginner. 10. In consulting the Grammar, the Index will be found of service for reference.
A FEW OF THE BOOKS MOST NECESSARY FOR THE BEGINNER.

The following list contains a few books that the beginner will find most useful. The list is very brief; the student as he advances will see how rapidly it may be enlarged.
a. Texts.

Geldner — *Avesta, or the Sacred Books of the Par sis.* — Stuttgart 1885 seq.

The new standard edition.

Westergaard — *Zendavesta, or the Religious Books of the Zoroastrians.* — Copenhagen.

Hard to procure, but useful until Geldner's edition is complete.

W. Geiger — *Aogemadaeca, ein Pdrsentract in Pdzend, Altbaktrisch und Sanskrit.*—Erlangen 1878.

Useful for the brief Av. fragment it contains.

Spiegel — *Die altpersischen Keilinschriften,* im Grundtexte mit Ubersetzung, Grammatik und Glossar. 2. Aufl. — Leipzig 1881.

Good for comparative purposes.
b. Dictionary.

Justi—*Handbuch der Zendsprache,* Altbaktrisches Worterbuch. — Leipzig 1864.

The only dictionary at present, and indispensable for reference. Possible to obtain second-hand.
c. Translation.

Darmesteter And Mills — *The Zend-Avesta* translated, in the *Sacred Books of the East,* ed. by F. Max Miiller, vols, iv, xxiii, xxxi. — Oxford 1883-7.

This translation is complete. Translations of separate portions are to be found in the works mentioned under (d) and (e).
d. Grammar and Exegesis, including also Translations of.selected portions. (Books specially mentioned above in Preface, are not repeated here.)

Bartholomae—*Arische Forschangen* i-iii. — Halle 1882-7.

Grammatical and metrical investigations, with translations of selected Passages.

Geldner — *Ueber die Metrik des jiingeren Avesta.* — Tubingen 1877.

A useful treatise on Metre. Also contains translations.

— *Studien zum Avesta.* — Strassburg 1882.

Grammatical contributions, and numerous translations.

— *Drei Yasht aus dent Zendavesta* tibersetzt und erklart. —Stuttgart 1884.

Translation of Yt. 14, 17, 19, with Commentary.

Spiegel—*Commentar tiber das Avesta.* Bd. i-ii.—Wien 1864-8.

Useful for occasional reference.
e. Literature, Religion, Antiquities.

Darab Peshotan Sanjana—*Civilization of the Eastern Iranians.* Vols, i-ii; being a translation from the German of W. Geiger's *Ostiranische Kultur im Alterthum.* — London 1885-6. Useful for reference.

Geldner—*Zend-Avesta, Zoroaster,* articles in the *Encyclopaedia Britannica.* Ninth edition.—1888. By all means to be consulted.

Haug And West—*Essays* on the Sacred Language, Writings, and Religion of the Parsis. 3 ed.—London 1884.

Contains much useful information.

Firoz Jamaspji — Casartelli's *Mazdayasnian Religion under the Sassanids.* — Bombay 1889.

Treats fully of the later development of Zoroastrianism.

Ragozin—*Media, Babylon and Persia.* (Story of Nations' Series.) —New York 1888.

A good and readable book.

Windischmann—*Zoroastrische Studien,* herausgegeben von
Fr. Spiegel.—Berlin 1863.
Contains much good material.

Beside the above works the student will find abundant and valuable contributions on the Avesta and kindred Iranian subjects in the philological journals and periodicals of the last few years. Reference need only be made to the names Bartholomae, Bang, Bezzenberger, Caland, Casartelli, Darmesteter, de Harlez, Geiger, Geldner, Horn, Hiibschmann, Fr. Miiller, Mills, Pischel, Spiegel, Wilhelm, and some others, in the following: *Bezzenberger s Beitrage; Kuhn's Zeitschrift; Zeitschrift der deutschen morgenlandischen Geseltschaft; Brugmann und Streitberg's Indogermanische Forschungen; Le Museon;*

Abbreviations. adj. = adjective advl.
= adverbial etc. = *et cetera*
et al. = *et alia*
fr. = from
indecl. = indeclinable infin. = infinitive
nom. propr. = *rumen proprium* num. =
numeral orig. = original, originally opp.
, opp. to = opposed to pret. = preterite
ptcpl. = participle str. = strong subst. =
substantive v. 1. = *varia lectio* var. —
variant wk. = weak.

The other abbrev

Observe.

1. A v. (Avesta) prefixed to a word indi-
cates that the word or form in question
is either found in both GAV. and YAV.
or has nothing peculiar about it which
would prevent its occurence in both. 2.
GAV. (Gatha Avesta) is prefixed (i)
when the word, or form, or construction
is peculiar to the Gatha dialect and is
not found in YAV.; (2) to contrast a
Gatha form with a younger form (YAV.
) which may stand beside it; (3) to emphasize the fact that the form in question is found even in the Gathas, e. g.
*stavas* § 143.
Under GAV. are comprised the usual 17
hymns and the sacred formulas (Introd.
p. xxiii, § 25), the Yasna Haptanghaiti,
and those portions, such as Ys. 12, that
are written in the Gatha dialect even including some possible later imitations,
e. g. Ys. 58, 4.26.
3. YAV. (Younger Avesta) comprises
everything that is not written in the dialect of the Gathas. For its usage see
preceding note. 4. The sign () is placed
before a form to denote that the first part
of the word is omitted. 5. In the paradigms under Inflection, the forms in
parentheses () do not actually occur, but
are made up after the form in small print
which stands beside them. See. § 236
foot-note. Thus
Loc. *(yasnae$u) viraliu.* GRAMMAR.
PHONOLOGY.
Alphabet.
§ 1. The Avesta is written in the following characters
A. Vowels.
§ 2. The writing runs from right to
left. The vowels are fully expressed by
individual letters as in Greek
Note. The epenthetic and anaptyctic
vowels (§§ 70, 72) will be expressed in
transcription, in the Grammar only, by
a small vowel slightly raised: e. g. A v.
*a"ru$a-*'white' = Skt. *arusd-;* Av. *an-
tar'* 'within'= Skt. *antar.* etc.; there are
no diacritical points; nor are any accents
written in the Avesta texts.
§ 3. In the manuscripts numerous ligatures occur; these except *&o St* are
generally resolved in printing. Observe
that e» *h* is different from »«. *hv.* Many
MSS. have a sign *m* interchanging with-
Gar *hm.*
§ 4. In Avesta, all words except some
enclitics are written separately and each
is followed by a point (.); the compounds even are mostly written separately in the MSS.; but in printed texts
these are written together, a point (.) being used to divide the members.
§ 5. The punctuation in the MSS. is
meagre, mostly arbitrary and quite ir-
regular; the following symbols borrowed from the MSS. have been adopted
to correspond to our signs, namely-.-for
colon or semicolon; v a full stop; op a
larger break; 0 0 the end of a chapter; «
symbol of abbreviation.
Pronunciation. § 6. Vowels. *i,-f i,* and
*u, $ u* are pronounced as ordinarily in
Sanskrit, but *a, a* perhaps duller. —*i 3*
is most probably obscure like the short
indefinite vowel familiar in English,
'gard«it?r', 'meas«ring', 'history',
'sachem'; it often corresponds to the
vulgar 'chimeney', 'rheumatisum'. In
the combination i *ar',* cf. Skt. *f,* much

like English 'pretty' (when pronounced 'peretty'), e. g. "vho p3r'saf 'he asked', cf. Mod. Persian *purstdan* 'to ask'; Av. *mar'ja*-'bird', Skt. *mrga*-, Mod. Pers. *murj*. See above, Introduction, on Transcription.—is the corresponding long vowel to ( *3*. —10 *e* and *e*, both narrow, about as English 'let, veil', French 'et£'. —*o* and *0* probably somewhat muffled. —*ce*, as English 'extraordinary, foalt, fawing', i. e. approaching '-aw' in 'saw', i— . *q*, nasalized *a*, or *a*, French 'sans', likely rather dull.

§ 7. Diphthongs. *ai* and *du* are pronounced as in Sanskrit. — *oi* as a Gk. cot. — *ao* and j « as a union of the two elements *ai* etc. — Ioj *ie* as forming two distinct sounds.

§ 8. Tenues *k*, *Y t*, « /, and Mediae c-£0 as ordinarily. — r *c, j*, as in Sanskrit, English 'church, judge'.

§ 9. Spirants, *b* , as *ch* in Scotch 'loch', Mod. Gk. *j*. — *j*, a roughened *g*, guttural buzz, cf. (often) Germ. 'Tage', Mod. Gk. y. — *6 J*, as English 'thin', surd.— *d*, as English 'then', sonant.— *f*, apparently a spirant, § 81.

— i /) as in English. — Qu w, corresponding sonant, Germ. *w*, Mod. Gk. p (cf. Eng. *v).* — u J, sharp as in'sister'. — / *z*, corresponding sonant, English 'zeal'.—-u *s*, as English *sh* in 'dash'. — u *i*, corresponding sonant, English 'pleasure, azure'.—ro *$*, a more palatal generally before*y*.

— ra *S*, apparently a variety *sh*, differing little from-o *s;* etymologically it most often equals original *rt*.

§ 10. Nasals, #, guttural = Skt. ».— *a q*, a modification of the preceding,-mouill£; the two (1 *w* and-u *v)* respectively perhaps as in Eng. 'longing'. — 1 *n*, as Eng. 'nun'.—£! u (modified from *an)*, a variety of *n*.—*4m*, as ordinarily.

§ 11. Semivowels and Liquid, *roy* (initial), probably spirant as Eng. 'youth'; — *y* (internal), probably semivowel, *i*, English 'many a man'. — *v* (initial), probably spirant as Eng. 'vanish'; —» *v* (internal), probably semivowel, *u*, cf. Eng. 'lower, flour'.—*r* is a liquid vigorously pronounced. Observe / is wanting.

Note. On » in *uvalbya*, see Vocabulary after *u*.

§ 12. Aspiration. & *h*, as ordinarily. — *fy*, a modification of *h* before *y*, possibly stronger.

§ 13. Ligature, *v k*, perhaps more vigorous than w *hv*, and possibly already shading towards the later Pers. *f*.
Sounds.

SYSTEM OF VOWELS. § 14. General Remark. The Avesta presents a greater variety than the Sanskrit in its vowelsystem, especially through the frequent presence of *e*-and *o*-sounds instead of *a*. Simple Vowels.

A. Agreement in Quality between Avesta and
Sanskrit Vowels.
Av. *3 1* —— v o
*a, i, u*, — *a, i, ii*. i. Agreement in both Quality and Quantity. §15. The Av. vowels *a, a, i, i, u, ii*, agree in general with the corresponding vowels in Sanskrit.
(1) Av. a = Skt. *a;*—Av. a = Skt. *a*. Av. *asti* 'is' = Skt. *dsti;* Av. *mataro* 'mothers' = Skt. *mdtdras;* Av. *vdtais* 'with winds'= Skt. *vatdis*. (2) Av. z = Skt *i;*—Av. f=Skt. *I*. Av. *cistis* 'wisdom' = Skt. *cittis;* Av. *hitica'ti* 'he sprinkles' = Skt. *sincdti;* Av. *jivyqm* 'living, fresh' (acc. f.) = Skt. *jivydm*. (3) Av. « = Skt. *u;*—Av. « = Skt. *it*. Av. *uta* 'also' = Skt. *utd;* Av. *dduru* 'wood' = Skt. *ddru;* — Av. *burdis* 'of richness' = Skt. *bhures;* Av. *bumim* 'earth' = Skt. *bhumim*. ii. Agreement in quality; difference in quantity.
§ 16. As to the relation between long and short quantity, the Avesta and the Sanskrit do not always coincide with each other. This is probably due in part to shifting of accent, partly to deficiencies or inaccuracy in Avesta writing, partly to dialectic peculiarities.

B. Differences in Quality between Avesta and Sanskrit
Vowels.
Av. (, , 10, ty '»,',— K", )C.
*3, S, e, e, o, 0,—m, q*.
§ 27. The above vowels are found under special conditions as representatives of Skt. *a* and *a*.
§ 28. Summary. The Av. *e* answers oftenest to Skt. *a* before *n* or *m*, also occasionally before *v*. It is commonly the anaptyctic vowel.—The corresponding long is j *S* very frequent in GAv., more

rare in YAV.—The letter R *e* is commonly a shading from *a* after J'.—The corresponding long is —Avesta 0 and J stand sometimes for *a* under influence of a labial, *u, v*.—Av. & is either Skt. flJ, or it answers to Skt. a before « plus stopsound.—Av. *x; q* is nasalization of *a, a* before *tn, n;* it often answers to Skt. *a* with anusvara.

Av. ( *3*.

§ 29. Av.,? often corresponds to Skt. *a* before *n* or *m*—regularly so before the latter when final; occasionally also before *v*.

Av. *vitidan* 'they found' = Skt. *dvindan;* Av. *hatitem* 'being' = Skt. *sdntam;* Av. *upamam* (beside *tipamani)* 'highest'= Skt. *upamdm;*—GAv. *evistl* 'by ignorance', cf. Skt. *dvitti;* Av. *ma'ny3vzm* 'spiritual' beside Av. *ma'nyavo;* Av. *s3vista*-'most mighty, beneficent' (beside *savo)* = Skt. *sdviftha*-; Av. *hvcwtovim* 'blessed life' Ys. 53.1 (acc. from *hvavhavya*-).

Note. The MSS. sometimes vary between *s* and *a:* e. g. Av. *barantd* beside *baritlt o* 'carrying'; *jasantu* beside *jasstitu* 'let them come'; *vazatiti* beside *vazstiti* 'they drive'; etc.

§ 30. The *3* (§ 29) arising from *a* before *tn* or *n*, is often palatalized to *i* when either *y, c, j* or *z*, immediately precedes.

Av. *yim* 'whom' = Skt. *yam;* Av. *vdcim* 'voice' beside *vdc3m = Skt. vacatn;* Av. *drujim* beside *druj3m* 'Deceit, Fiend' = Skt. *druhatn;* Av. *bujim* beside *bujam* 'absolution'; Av. *bajina* 'dishes' = Skt. *bhdjana*-; Av. *drazimno* 'holding' beside Av. *drazantnd*.

§ 31. In GAv., *B* appears sometimes to be written (as a kind of dissimilation) for *u* or *i*, when in the following syllable an *u (v)* or *i* stands. The epenthetic vowel is written beside it, according to rule § 70. Thus is to

Original *r* (r-sonant).

Av. *ar», (ars)* = Skt. r§ 47. The Skt. *r* is represented in Av. by *W* or often *ar'*.
Concurrence of vowels.

Contraction and Resolution.' § 50. General Remark. In Avesta, the rule for the union of two vowels within a word or in composition, corresponds in general to the Sanskrit, (i) Two similar vowels coalesce into their corresponding long (sometimes short). (2) Two dissimilar vowels, when the first is *a* unite in giving guna § 60. (3) Before dissimilar vowels, the *i*-or «-vowel (simple or in diphthongs), passes over into the corresponding semi-vowel. (4) In Avesta compounds, however, hiatus is often allowed to remain.

Diphthongs.

§53. General Remark. The Avesta vowel-combinations (diphthongs with triphthongs) are of four-fold origin, and may conveniently be divided and designated as follows: i. Proper diphthongs, corresponding to Sanskrit *guna* (more rarely *vrddhi*) in its two-fold sense: (1) vowelstrengthening, (2) the result of contraction of two dissimilar vowels. See § 60 seq. ii. Re duct ion-diphthongs, resulting from reduction by contraction of two syllables. See § 64 seq. Metrically often dissyllabic. iii. Improper diphthongs (and triphthongs) arising from epenthesis. See § 70 seq. iv. Protraction-diphthong *da,* a peculiar extension of *a* or *d* into *da* in ablative singular before *-ca* 'que'; likewise in *daf* 'then' (abl. as adv. ), GAv. *bdaf* 'verily' Ys. 35.5. Cf. Av. *daevdafca* 'and from the Demon' *(daeva-);* *apdafca* beside *apaf* 'from water', etc.

Proper Diphthongs.

Av. (", —g —-"", *ae, di*— *ao, 9u* — *di, du.* § 54. The above are real diphthongs when they correspond to the Skt. diphthongs. The relation between the Av. and the Skt. diphthongs is concisely this: a. Skt. *e* is represented in Av. (1) chiefly by *ae,* (2) less often by *di,* (3) again by *e,* only when final, but there regularly, p. Skt. *0* is represented in Av. (1) chiefly by *ao,* (2) more rarely by *Su,* (3) again by *0,* only when final, but there regularly, y. Skt. *di* and *du* are represented in Av. by *di* and *du.*

Note. In some instances Skt. *Su* (final) seems to be represented in Av. by *a,* § 42.

Av. *ae* = Skt. */.* § 55. The diphthong Av. *ae* (very common) answers to Skt. *e* (old *at),* initial or internal; likewise as ending in first member of a compound, or again before enclitic *-ca* 'que' *tdyos.*

— Av. *fraotd* 'pronounced' *(fra + w)* = Skt. *proktds.*

Note. On reduction-diphthong *ao,* see § 64.

Av. *iu* = Skt. *0.* § 58. The diphthong Av. *iu* (as strengthening of «), also sometimes answers to Skt. *0,* internal. It occurs in the genitive of a-stems, and in a very few words. Observe the pair *Su* and *ao* as *oi* and *ae.*

Av. *tyratius* 'of wisdom' = Skt. *krdtos;* Av. *vawhSus* 'of the good' = Skt. *vdsos;* Av. *mafny3us* 'of spirit' = Skt. *manyds.*—Also in *dSus.sravm* 'things of illrepute', cf. *haosravawha;* *dSus. manahya-* 'evil-minded', cf. *haomanavha-;* GAv. *giu$ais* 'with ears' = Skt. *gho$dis.*

Av. *at* = Skt. *at;*—Av. *au* = Skt. *du.* § 59. Av. *at, du* when they are real diphthongs (i. e. not epenthetic or reduction) correspond to Skt. *di, du.* Av. *mqprdis* 'with words' = Skt. *mdntrdis;* Av. *gdus* (nom.) 'cow' = Skt. *gdus.* i. Vowel-Strengthening — a-Vowel Contraction. § 60. Guna and Vrddhi. The terms *guna* and *vrddhi* are conveniently borrowed from the Sanskrit Grammar for the Avesta. In Avesta, as in Sanskrit, guna-and vrddhivowels in the fullest sense have a double origin: (1) vowelstrengthening in vowel-gradation;1 (2) contraction of two dissimilar vowels whether in composition.or in inflection.

Brugmann, *Grundriss der vergl. Gram.* § 307 seq.

Guna in Avesta, owing to the greater richness in the vowel system, has a greater variety than in Sanskrit.— The vrddhi-increment, however, is comparatively rare, and is not so regularly carried out as in Sanskrit; nor are the instances always certain (cf. § 18 Note 1); but vrddhi is not to be denied to the Avesta.

Synopsis of Guna and Vrddhi modelled after the Sanskrit.

Avesta.

Simple Vowel. *a, a i i, i u, u* I *ir' ae (ay), oi (dy),-e ao (av), iu,-o ar' (ar) Si (ay) au (av) ar' (ar)* (The forms in parentheses appear before vowels. On the interchange of *ae, oi,* see § 56).

'looking around' *(fdi)* = Skt. *didivan;* perhaps A v. *JajmxS* 'having smitten'

cf. Skt. *jagknivdn.*

Note 3. Internal *ay, av* are sometimes found written as an extension of *y, v* (i. e. *iy, uv):* Av. *nSvaya-* 'navigable, flowing' = Skt. *nSvya;* Av. *aspaya-* (cf. acc. *aspaem* § 64) 'belonging to a horse' = Skt. *divya-;* Av. *hava-* (cf. gen. f. *haoy-ai)* 'suus' = Skt. *sva-;* Av. *kava* variant for *kva* 'where' = Skt. *hva.* iii. Epenthesis, Prothesis, and Anaptyxis.

Cf. Brugmann, *Grundriss der vergl. Grammatik* § 637 seq.; § 623 seq.

§ 69. Two of these viz. Epenthesis, Prothesis (and certain cases of Anaptyxis like *s"runvatd)*—may be considered fundamentally the same, as each consists in the introduction of an anticipatory parasitic sound. For convenience, however, in the following, Epenthesis and Prothesis will be distinguished thus: (1) Epenthesis—an anticipatory vowel attached internally to a vowel; (2) Prothesis—an anticipatory vowel attached initially before a consonant.

§ 70. Epenthesis is one of the characteristic soundphenomena of the Avesta. It consists in the insertion of a light anticipatory *i* or *u,* when in the following syllable respectively an *i, t, e, e, y,* or an *u, v* stands.—Epenthesis of *i* takes place before *r, n, tit, t, p, pr, d, p, b, w,* also before *fgh* (= orig. *sy).*—Epenthesis of *u* takes place only before *r.*

Note. The epenthetic vowel attaches itself parasitically to diphthongs as well as to the simple vowels including a-privative. In the MSS., the law of epenthesis is not always consistently carried out; many times it is omitted: e. g. *manySul* beside *ma 'nyiul* 'of the Spirit'.

Epenthetic /.

Av. *bava 'ti* 'he becomes' = Skt. *bhdvati;* Av. *ae 'ti* (GAv. *ae 'ti)* 'he goes' = Skt. *iti;* Av. *ina&ti* 'he forces, drives' = Skt. *inoti;* Av. *a 'pi* 'unto, in' = Skt. *dpi;* Av. *bara 'titi* 'they carry' = Skt. *bh-dranti;* Av. *a 'nik3tn* 'face' = Skt. *dri-ikam;* Av. *bufri* 'fullness'= Skt. *bhuri;* Av. *airistem* 'unhurt' = Skt. *driffam.* — GAv.

SYSTEM OF CONSONANTS.

§ 73. General Remark. Viewing the Av. and the Skt. system of consonants side by side, it may be noted: (1) The Av. palatal series is incomplete—-the Av.

possesses only *c* and *j*. (2) The Skt. cerebral series is entirely wanting in the Avesta. (3) The Av. has no aspirates, their place being in part taken by the corresponding spirants. (4) The nasals are only in part identical. (5) The Av. is richer than the Skt. in sibilants, especially through the presence of the sonant sibilants *z* and *z*. intermediate between *t, d* and *p, d*. It is both surd and sonant (voiceless and voiced); to find a distinction palaeographically when it appears as surd or as sonant is not warranted by the MSS. It occurs chiefly as final for *t*, except when *s* or *s* precede; in that case *t* appears § 192. As initial, surd and sonant, it is found in a few words, *kaepm* 'faith, faithful'; *bae$o* 'hatred, harm' = Skt. *dvi$as*, cf. § 96. As internal it occurs in a few words, compound or in the MSS. treated as compound, and therefore handled as if it were final.

§ 74. Surd and Sonant (Voiceless and Voiced). For the distinction between surd and sonant (voiceless and voiced), we may refer to the Sanskrit. The law, moreover, that in internal combination, surd (voiceless) consonants stand before surd consonants, and sonant (voiced) before sonants, has in general the same extent as in Sanskrit.1 Observe that *n* and in part *m* are at times treated as surd.2 § 75. Sandhi between words (§ 4) is wanting in Avesta, except in case of some enclitics and compounds.

Tenues — Surd Spirants.

Av. 9, 10 u and *r* — *lr*, 6, *i* £.

*k, t, p* and *c* — *ft, p, f* — /.

Av. *k, t, p* and *c*. § 76. The Av. tenues *k, t, p* and *c* agree mostly with the corresponding tenues in the Sanskrit.

Av. *katard* 'which of two' = Skt. *katards;* Av. *tdpaye'ti* 'makes hot' = Skt. *tapdyati;* Av. *pat3titi* 'they fly' = Skt. *pdtanti.*—Av. *cara'ti* 'he moves' = Skt. *cdrati;* Av. *cakana* 'has been pleased' = Skt. *cdkana.*

Note. In the distinction between guttural and palatal *k/c*, the Av. and the Skt. do not always agree: Av. *paskSt* 'from behind, behind' = Skt. *pascat*, cf. Av. *fiasco;* Av. *cicipwa* 'through the wise one' = Skt. *eikitvd;* Av. *frald.car'tar-* 'converter'= Skt. *kartar-*, cf. A v. *frald. kir'ti';* Av. *vaoku$e* dat. sg. pf. ptcpl.

*fvakc* = Skt. *ucuse.*

Av. *fy P /*

§ 77. The surd spirants *ft, p, f* in Av. are of two-fold origin: — (1) they are the representatives 1 Cf. Whitney, *Sanskrit Grammar*, § 156 seq.; Stenzler, *Elementarbuck der Sanskritsprache*, § 44 seq.

! See Sievers, *Grundzuge der Phonetik*, pp. 114, 133.

Av. *aa;dp* 'from Right' = Skt. *rtdt;* Av. *bavaf* 'he became' = Skt. *dbhavat;* Av. *yavaf* 'how much' = Skt. *ydvat;* Av. *hakar3f* 'once' = Skt. *sakft.*— GAV. *haecaf.aspa*-nom. propr.; YAV. *a"rvaf.aspa-* 'swifthorsed'; Av. *brvafbyqm* 'both brows'; Av. *tafkufis* 'running' (MSS. *taf ku$is);* Av. *afca* 'atque'.— GYAV. *fkaepm* 'faith, faithful'; YAV. *fiae$d* 'hatred, harm', cf. GAV. *dvae$awhd* = Skt. *dvesas.*

Note 1. Sometimes, / appears as variant of *d* before *k:* e.g. *adkitn* 'robe' (variant *a(kim)* = Skt. *dtkam.*

Note 2. In *ta(.Sp)nt* 'with running water' (adj.), Yt. 13.43, / stands for final *c*, cf. Av. *taci a'pya* 'in running water' (loc.), Vd. 6.26.

Mediae — Sonant Spirants.

Av. *c, j, _j* and *g;* — *l,, t, m.*

*g, d, b* and *j* — *j, d, w.*

§ 82. The mediae *g, d, b*, in Av. have a two-fold value:—(1) they represent old mediae, agreeing with the Skt. *g, d, b;* or (2) they are the representatives of the old sonant aspirates, *gh, dh, bh;* that is to say, originally in Av. the sonant aspirates lost their aspiration and fell together with the mediae. In GAV., the mediae thus arising are regularly preserved unchanged throughout. But see § 82 (a).

The following scheme shows the standpoint of the Gat has in comparison with the Sanskrit.

Skt *g gh d dh b bh*

V V V

Original-and GAV. *g d b* (1) GAV. (old) *g, d, b* = Skt. *g, d, b.* GAV. *ugrStig* 'mighty' (acc. pl.) = Skt. *ugrdn;*— GAV. *yada* 'when' = Skt. *yadd;* GAV. *vidvat* 'knowing' = Skt. *vidvdn.* (2) GAV. *g, d, b* = Skt. *gh, dh, bh.* GAV. *dar'gSm* 'long' = Skt. *dirghdm;*—GAV. *add* 'then' = Skt. *ddha;* GAV. *advamtn* 'way' = Skt. *ddhvdnam;*—GAV. *uboibyd* 'both', cf.

Skt. *ubhdbhydm;* GAV. *a'bi* 'unto' = Skt. *abhl.*

§ 82 a. Observe in connection with this rule § 82 that the sonant spirants appear before *z:* cf. § 180. GAV. *aojzd* 'thou spakest'; *diwza'dydi.*—See § 89 Bartholomae's Law.

Note. On the sonant spirants—in GAV. *raftdra-*'aid'; *ufrta-*'spoken, word'—arising from old tenues or aspirate tenues, cf. § 77 Note 3.

§ 83. (1) In YAV. these mediae *g, d, b*—of double origin § 82—are preserved unchanged when initial; or again when internal, if immediately preceded by a nasal consonant or by a sibilant. (2) Under all other circumstances in YAV. these mediae—whether representing old mediae or old sonant aspirates—are regularly changed to the corresponding sonant spirant *Q, d, w).* Exceptions to the rule are not many. The secondary relation of GAV. to YAV. may thus be tabulated (cf. § 82): GAV. *g d t* AAA YAV. *g j d d b w*

Sibilants.

Av. i),-o, gj, ro—/, «u.

if tf % § 106. General Remark. Of the sibilants, *s, s, f, $* are surd; and *z, z* are sonant. In Avesta, *s* corresponds to both Skt. *s* and to *s*.—Av. / answers in general to Skt. The letter Av. *s* is chiefly final after *i, u* and consonants, also in some ligatures. Av. / is not so common, chiefly before *y.*

Note. Av. /, /, / are palaeographically closely related. In most MSS., / and / interchange with each other. In the younger Indian MSS., / is the predominant character; the Persian MSS. often (though by no means throughout) show a preference for / when the sound answers to orig. *rt*. In the four oldest MSS. , with Pahlavi translation, / is the principal character,—/ standing as final or in ligatures. This rule is there preserved almost without exception.—In the old Mss. ro/has a double value—(1) as a ligature for/-(-, *hilku* 'dry', et al.; or (2) it is a modification of /, / before *y*, § 162. Younger MSS. write in the (1) first case *Ik;* in the (2) second case they have a special ligature.—See Geldner, *Drei Yasht* p. viii seqq.

Av. *s.*

§107. General Remark. Av. *s* is of three-fold origin:— 1. = original *s*, 2. = older palatal *s* (Skt. *s*), 3. = developed. 1. Original *s*. § 108. General Remark. Original *s* (1) under certain conditions remains *s* in Avesta (2) but generally otherwise becomes *h (vh)*. i. Original *s* remains *s*. § 109. Original *s* remains *s* in Avesta before initial *k, c, t,p,n,* or internal before the same letters when it is preceded by *a, a*.

Original Av. z changed to *s, /*. § 172. Av. 2 before « becomes *s Q)*, see §§ 153, 164 for examples. § 173. Av. 2 before *m* becomes *s*, see § 152 examples. § 174. Av. 2 before / becomes *l*, see § 166 examples. § 175. Av. 2 before *s* becomes /, see § 165 examples.

Resum6.

Principal differences between Sanskrit and Avesta in Phonology.

Vowels.

§ 195. GAv. lengthens all final vowels, YAv. lengthens them in monosyllables, shortens them in polysyllables (§§ 24—26).

§ 196. Original *t* and *u* are lengthened before final *m* in A v. (§ 23).

§ 197. Av. ( *s* generally answers to Skt. *a* before *m* or «. — Av. *,r» (ar 'J =* Skt. *r* (§§ 29. 47)

§ 198. Av. K commonly a modification of internal *a* after *y.*— Sometimes equals final *ya* (§§ 34, 67).

§ 199. A v. "t» *d* chiefly equals final Skt. *as (d)* § 120.

§ 200. A v. p" *a* chiefly equals Skt. *as;* — more rarely Skt. *S* -(stop-sound (§§ 121 —124, 44).

§ 201. Av. r? is a nasalization of *a (a)* before *m* or *n*. It often equals Skt. *a* with anusvara (§§ 45, 46).

Diphthongs.

§ 202. The Skt. *e* is represented by Av. *al, oi,* or (when final) *e;* the Skt. *o* by Av. *ao, iu,* or (when final) *d* (§§ 55— 58, 35, 41).

§ 203. A striking peculiarity in Av. is Epenthesis (§ 70) and Anaptyxis (§ 72) and the frequent Reductions (samprasarana etc.) § 63 seq.

Consonants.

§ 204. The voiceless spirants A v. *fi, p, /* are chiefly sprung from old tenues *k, t, p* before consonants; — sometimes they represent old voiceless aspirates (§ 77 seq.).

§ 205. The original voiced aspirates *gh, dh, bh* fell primarily together with the mediae in Av. (§ 82).

§ 206. The voiced spirants Av. *j, d, w* are developments from these earlier two-fold mediae (§ 83).

§ 207. Skt. *j* is often represented by Av. 2 (§ 168).

§ 208. Skt. *h* is represented sometimes by Av. *j*, sometimes by

Av. *z* (§§ 88, 169).

§ 209. Skt. *s* generally becomes *h* in Av. (§ 110 seq.).

§ 210. Skt. *as* (internal) becomes *avh, ah;* or (final) *o* (§§ in —120).

§ 211. Av. *as* (internal) becomes *a?vh, ah;* or (final) *a* (§§ 121—124).

§ 212. Skt. *s* is represented in Av. by *s* (§ 146).

§ 213. Skt. *sv* is represented in Av. by *sp* (§ 97).

§ 214. Skt. *ch* is represented in A v. by *s* (§ 142).

§ 215. Dentals before dentals are changed to *s* in Av. (§ 151).

§ 216. Av. *z* and *s* (= Skt. *s)* before voiceless consonants generally become / (§§ 164—166, 160).

§ 217. Skt. *rt* is often represented in Av. by / (§ 163).

§ 218. Skt. *ks* is represented by Av. or / (§ 158 Note 1).

INFLECTION.

DECLENSION,

NOUNS AND ADJECTIVES.

§ 219. Nominal declension includes nouns and adjectives; these may be conveniently taken together in Avesta and divided into two great classes of declension—(a) the vowel class, and (b) the consonant class—according as the stem ends in a vowel or in a consonant.

For a summary of Avesta declension in a tabular form, see opposite page.

§ 220. Case, Number, Gender. The Avesta agrees with the Sanskrit in its eight cases, nominative, accusative, instrumental, dative, ablative, genitive, locative, vocative; three numbers, singular, dual, plural; and in the three genders, masculine, feminine, and neuter.

The uses of the cases are in general the same as in Skt. but see § 233. The Av. dual is interesting as showing a distinct form for the locative case, see §§ 223, 236, 262. In Avesta, a substantive has commonly the same gender that it has in Sanskrit.

Note 1. As to gender, however, some individual peculiarities occur, as a few words in Av. show a different gender from that which they have in Skt.:— e. g. Av. *vac*-(masc.) 'vox' = Skt. *vde* (fem.)—but observe the compound *pa 'tivac*-is fem.; Av. *tar$na*-(masc.) 'thirst' = Skt. *tfsm*(fem.); Av. *zanga*-(masc.) 'leg' = Skt. *javgha*-(fem.); Av. *sti*-(fem.) 'existence, creation' = Skt. *sti*-(masc.) — This occasional phenomenon is sometimes important to observe in the matter of exegesis.

Note 2. On fem. and neut. plur. forms interchanging with each other, see § 232.

6. (A) Stems without suffix. 7. (B) Derivative stems in *-atit,-matit,-vatit.* 8. (C) Derivative stems in *-an,-man,-van.* 9. (D) Derivative stems in *-in.* 10. (E) Radical stems in-« and *-m*. a. Derivative stems in original *-tar,-ar.* b. Radical stems in original *-r. c.* Neuters (derivative) in original *-ar.* 11 (F) Stems in original *r* 11 (G) Stems in original f b. Radical stems in *-h* (original *-s)*— j "f 1 e IP-Th c. Derivative stems in *-uL* Those resembling them.

§ 221. Endings. Here may be enumerated the normal endings which are added to the stem in formation of the various cases. The stem itself, moreover, sometimes varies in assuming these endings, as it often appears in a stronger form in certain cases, and in a weaker form in others. Connecting elements as in Skt. seem at times to be introduced between stem and ending.

The normal endings (but observe §§ 25, 26) are: i. MASCULINE—FEMIN INE.

General Remarks on the Endings.

i. MASCULINE —FEMINISE. § 222. Singular:—

Nominative: The typical ending *-s* is disguised by entering into euphonic combinations with vowels and consonants; it assumes especially often the form § 156. — Often it is wanting—e.g. cf. derivative stems in orig. *S* and *i*.

Accusative: The typical ending *-«t*

appears after vowels; the ending *-im* (= *-am* = *-mm*) after consonants. Cf. also § 23.

Instrumental: Regularly *a, a,* § 25.— This is sometimes disguised by combining with a preceding *y* to *e,* § 67.—The fem, a-declension, as in Skt., shows a fuller form, making the case end in *-aya (-aya)* beside the simpler normal form in *a.*

Dative: YAV. *-e* (orig. *-at),* GAV. *-i,-oi,* § 56.—Notice of course Av. *-ae-ca.* — In the a-declension, the *e* (orig. *at)* unites with the stem vowel into *Si,* cf. Gr. p, § 60. — The feminine derivative a-stems and z-stems show a fuller ending *Si,* which in the a-stems is preceded by a *y,* as in Skt. also.

Ablative: The typical ending is-/, or *-(a)(* (consonant deck), *-at* (in a-decl.). Observe, this is not confined, as in Skt. , simply to the *a*declension, but appears in all the declensions *(a, I, a* and cons. ). Instances of interchanges between -*a(* and *-S(* are not infrequent.— Observe before *-ca,* the form *-Satca,* § 53 iv.— The ending *-(a)(* is often followed by the enclitic postposition *a,* thus giving -*(a)da.*—In GAV., the */-*ablative is found, as in Skt., only with the a-declension, e. g. *$afra(, aka(;* otherwise, as in Skt., the genitive is used with ablative force. — The feminine *a*-and r-stems, unlike the Skt., both show *-S(* which in the a-stems is preceded by *y.*

Genitive: The common ending, as in Skt, is *d,-asca;* it occurs chiefly in the consonant declension.—The ending, simple *(s) /* is also found, e. g. throughout the i-and «-stems, the stem vowel being generally strengthened before it. —In the a-stems, the ending *-he* (Skt. *-sya,* § 67), GAV. *-hya,-ZiyScS* (on cf. § 133) is regularly found. — In feminine *S*-and i-stems a fuller ending *-&,-asca (* = Skt. *as)* is found, which in the 5-declension is preceded by *y* as in Skt.— see dative above.

Locative: The normal form, as in Skt. , is-».—In the a-declension, this coalesces with the stem vowel to *-e,-aeca.*—Sometimes the loc. is without ending—the stem being simply strengthened, e. g. cf. «-stems and some a«-forms.—To the locative ending, an en-

clitic postpositive *a* is often attached, giving rise to forms in *-ya (-aya), -ava.* —The feminine a-stems show *-aya* (perhaps orig. instr., or *ya*suffix advl.) answering to Skt. *-aySm.* Vocative: Commonly, simple stem without ending. — Often the nom. stands instead of the vocative. § 223. Dual:—

Nom. Acc. Voc.: The prevailing form for the consonant and the *a*declension is *S (a),* cf. Vedic Skt. *S.*—The a-stems show *e (e).*—The masc. fem. *i*-and «-stems simply lengthen (then YAV., cf. § 25 and Note, shorten) their stem vowels.

Instr. Dat. Abl.: The normal ending in Av. is *-byS (-bya).*—The *iona-byqm,* which exactly corresponds to Skt. -*bhyam,* is only once found, in Av. *br-vafiyqm* 'both brows'.—Instead of YAV. *-bya,* the form written *-we* (§§ 67, 87) often appears.

Genitive: Regularly *-£&,-asca* answering to Skt. *-ds*—a preceding vowel being treated as in Skt.

Locative: The ending *6* occurs in *zas-tayo* (YAV.) from *zasta-*'hand', in *uboyo* (GAV.) from *uba-*'both', and *avhvo* (GAV.) Ys. 41.2 from *avhu-*'world, life'. § 224. Plural:—

Nom. Voc.: The typical form orig. *as* occurs both in the vowel and the consonant classes of declension.—But beside this, in the masculine of both classes the ending *5 (a)* is common, especially in YAV.—Its occurrence in the consonant, declension is probably due to borrowing from the a-decl.—In the a-declension, the normal orig. *-as* unites, as in Skt., with the stem vowel, thus giving *-C6* (= orig. *-Ss,* § 124) which is, however, less common than the ending *a (a).*—Often the a-stems have *-Ssvho,* cf. Vedic Skt. -*Ssas.*—In the f-stems, the usual nom. pl. , as in Vedic Skt., is *-il* instead of *-yd,-yasca.*

Accusative: The original ending *-ns* (seen in *-qsca* from a-stems) appears in the consonant stems as *-d,-as* (i. e. orig. *-ns).*—Beside this, in the masculine of both classes the ending *a(a)s* found, cf. nom. above. — In the a-declension the normal orig. *-ns* combines with the *a* of the stem into YAV. *-q(n),-qsca,* GAV. *-ing,-qsca*—sometimes also YAV. *-i,-ilea.*—The fem. a-stems show-d, *-asca.*

—The masc. fem. *i*-and «-stems show generally *-ul.*

Instrumental: Everywhere the ending *-Hl,-bil* (§21 Note), except in the a-stems which show *-SiS.*

Dat. Abl.: The regular form is *-byd,-byasca,* or written *-wyo,-vyd,-uyd,* §§ 83 (4), 87, 62 Note 3.

Genitive: Universally *-qm,* which is often dissyllabic as in Vedic Skt. —In the vowel stems an « is usually inserted before this *-qm.*

Locative: The normal form is *-hu, -/«.* —To this ending, an enclitic postpositive *a* in YAV. is often attached, thus giving *-hva,-$va,* cf. Skt. *v&nifv a* RV. 9. 62.8.

H. NEUTER (Separate Forms). The neuter shows in general the same endings as the masculine. Its special forms, however, are worthy of note in the following cases:

§ 225. Singular:— Nom, A c c. V o c.: In general no ending — the case is simply the bare stem in its weak form, if the stem have a weak form. The a-stems have *m* as in the accusative masculine. § 226. Dual:—

Nom. Acc. Voc.: The ending orig. -*t* is to be recognized in the a-stems, where it is combined with the stem vowel preceding it, into *e,* e. g. *duy-e sa't-e* 'two hundred'. —Sometimes the simple stem (or like nom. sing.) seems to be used, e. g. *va, dqma* Yt. 15.43, 'two eyes' Yt. 11.2. § 227. Plural:—

Nom. Acc. Voc.: Commonly the ending is wanting i.e. the case-form is the simple stem, or if consonantal it is the strongest form of the stem (cf. *afsman-ivqn* i. e. orig. *Snt;* or again *mana* from a-stem). — Seldom the ending is *-i: nSmsni,* cf. Skt. *namSni.* — Sometimes in the consonant declension, the endings *-a,-a* of the vowel *(a*or *S-)* declension are found, cf. § 234, e. g. *daemana, masana, malsma* to stems *dalman-*'eye, glance', *masan-*'greatness', *malsman*'urine', but see § 308. § 228. General Plural Case.

The plural in Av. occasionally shows a certain instability which is exhibited in the transfer or rather generalization of some of its case-forms. This is especially true of the neuter plural; and in general it may be added that the tendency to fluctuation increases in proportion to the lateness of the text.—See also, Johannes Schmidt, *Pturalbitdungen der indogermanischen Neutra* pp. 259 seq., 98 seq.

§ 229. (1) The instrumental plural in *-bit,-Sil* is occasionally used in YAV. as general plural case, e.g. *azdbil* (as acc. neut. Vd. 6.49)— *vispSil* (nom. Yt. 8. 48), *sralltSil* (Yt. 22.9), *hrafstrSil* (as acc. Ys. 19.2), etc.

§ 230. (2) The an-stems have also the neuter plural in *q(n)* sometimes usea as general plural case, see § 308.

§ 231. (3) An ending-»/,-«/ (like orig. fem. pl.) is sometimes employed in nouns and adjectives as general plural case, acc. as well as instr., e.g. GYAV. *namintl* (as acc.) Yt. 1.11 and (as instr. ) Ys. 51.22 = Ys. 15.2, YAV. *aŞaonil* Vsp. 21.3, *savavha'ttl!* Vd. 19.37; *vavhuSVsp.* 6.1, GAV. *avavhul* (as instr. ) Ys. 12.4, *yatitf* Ys. 12.4.

§ 232. Interchange of Neuter with Feminine forms.

Closely connected with this instability in the plural (especially neuter) is the interchange between neuter and feminine forms, as the neuter plural (occasionally also the singular) often shows the closest analogy to the feminine. Instances of this interchange are abundant, e.g. a-d e c 1. *nmamm* (nom. acc. sg. neut.) 'house', beside which *nmanm* (acc. pl., cf. fem.), *nmanahu* (loc. pl., cf. fem.); *awr3m* (nom. acc. sg. neut.) 'cloud', *awrce* (nom. pl., cf. fem.).—o-stem *avawho* (gen. sg.) 'of aid', GYAV. *avahjdi* (dat. sg. fem.).— Similarly stem *bar'zah-*(neut.) beside *bar'za-*'height', et al. —Adjective combinations *tiŞaro sata* 'three hundred', *vispa. hu karŞvohu*'in all climes', *rasca'titis hrarspa* 'steaming viands'. See also, Johannes Schmidt, *Pluralbildungen* p. 29 seq.

§ 233. Interchange of cases in their functions. The cases in their usage are not always so sharply distinguished in YAV. as in Sanskrit. Sometimes a case may take upon itself the functions that belong properly to another, e. g. dative in genitive sense, etc. A discussion of the question, however, belongs to Syntax.

§ 234. Transition in Declension. Transfers of inflection in parts of some words from one declension to another, especially in general from the consonant declension to the -declension, are not infrequent in Avesta. A word may thus follow one declension in the majority of its cases, but occasionally make up certain of its forms quite after another declension. Examples are numerous and are of two kinds.

(a) The simple unchanged stem is used, but given the endings of another declension—much the commonest case, e.g. stem*j:a'dyatit-*'imploring' with dat. sg. *ja'dyatit-di* (o-decl.) instead of *ja'dyatit-e; tacitit-qm* acc. sg. f., et al.

(b) The stem itself is remodelled and made to conform to another declension, thus really giving a new stem, e. g. *sravah-*'word' with instr. pl. *sravais* (stem *srava-*) instead of *sravSbis* cf. gen. pl. *sravavhqm.* The case is much less common.

§ 235. Stem-gradation. In Avesta, as in Sanskrit— cf. Whitney, *Skt. Gram.* §311—the stem of a noun or adjective, especially in the consonant declension, often shows vowel-variation, strongest, middle or strong, and weak forms, *a, a,—, -ay-,-ay-,-i-; -au-,-ao-,-u-; -ar3-,- ar3-,-r-,-ar3-; -att-,-3tit-,-at-=nt; -an-,- 3n-,-n-;* etc. (cf. § 60). The strong and strongest forms appear commonly in Singular Nom. Acc. Loc., in Dual Nom. Ace, and in Plural Nom., of the Masc. and Fem., and in the Plural Nom. Acc. of the Neuter. The remaining cases are weak, but there is much overlapping in this matter of stemgradation. The distinctions are not always so sharply drawn as in Sanskrit.

A. STEMS IN VOWELS,

i. Stems in *a.*

Masculine and Neuter (cf. Whitney, *Skt. Gram.* § 330).

i. MASCULINE.

§ 236. Av.-"iwro *yasna-*m. 'worship, sacrifice' = Skt. *yajnd-.*

Av. *mazda-yasna-,1 daeva-yasna-1* 'worshipper of Mazda, of Demons'; *ahura-*'Lord, Ahura'; *vira-*'man'; *haoma-*'haoma-plant'.

1 The forms with e. g. *"yasna* are from

*mazda-yasna-, daeva-yasna-.* The forms in parentheses do not actually occur, but are made up after the forms beside them — so throughout below. Forms to be observed in GAV. and YAV.

§ 238. In general, GAV. has the same forms as above, with long final vowel, cf. § 26.

Forms to be observed in GAV. and YAV.

§ 244. In general, GAV. has the same forms as above, with the long final vowel, cf. § 26.

§ 245. Singular:— Nom.: YAV. also *na're* 'manly' (fem. adj., *-e =-ya,* § 67) = Skt. *ndrya.*— 1 See Haug, *Zand-Pahlavi Glossary* p. 100 1. 23.

B. Radical Stems in *a.*

§ 248. Stems with radical *a,* so far as they have not gone over to the ordinary *a, a* declension, are represented by a few forms (a) masculine and neuter, (b) feminine.

(i) Masculine and Neuter (cf. Lanman, *Noun Inflection in the Veda* p. 443 seq.). § 249. Declension of Av. *rapalStS-*m. 'warrior standing in chariot' = Skt. *rathlffhd-*(part of its forms, however, are from the stem *rapalStar-,* cf. Skt. *savyeffhdr-*).—The forms from radical *rapal-StS-*are: — Singular. Nom. *rapalSta;* Acc. *rapalHqm;* Dat. *rapoiSte* (cf. Skt. *dhiyq-dhi,* and on *oi* cf. § 56), *rapalStSi* (o-decl., cf. Skt. *rathlffhdyS*); Gen. *rapaeSta.*— Plural. Acc. *rapalStms-cS.*

Note 1. The forms from stem *rapalUar-*are enumerated at § 330.

Note 2. Similar, dat. sg. neut. *poi* 'for protecting'; cf. also *voi.*

Forms to be observed in GAV. and YAV. § 258. In general, GAV. has the same forms as above, with the long final vowel, cf. § 26. § 259. Singular:—

On varying *1, i* see § 21 Note 1. Nom. : GAV. has *aŞauni* Ys. 53.4.

Instr.: So GAV. *vavhuya* 'with good', *vahehya* 'with better', and *ma'nya* 'with thought', cf. Dat. *ma'nySi* Ys. 43.9. 1 Yt. 5.54, uncertain, cf. § 68 Note 3.

B. Derivative Stems in original *u.* (Cf. Whitney, *Skt. Gram.* § 356.) These are not sharply to be distinguished from A in Avesta, nor are they numerous. As example may be taken FEMININE.

§ 271. Av.-i-"»o *tanti*-f. 'body' = Skt. *tanu*-.

Forms to be observed in GAV. and YAV. § 272. Metrically, the *v* in *tanvSm* etc. is to be resolved into *u* as in Sanskrit.

1 See *AogamadaicS* 48 p. 25 ed. W. Geiger. B. STEMS IN CONSONANTS.

6. (A) Stems without Suffix.

Root-words and those inflected like them.

Masculine, Feminine and Neuter (cf. Whitney, *Skt. Gr.* §§383, 391).

§ 279. Av. -*w vis*-f. 'village' = Skt. *vis*-.

Av. *spas*-m. 'spy', *amir'tSt*-f. 'Immortality', *asI*-n. 'bone', *nas* 7. (B) Derivative Stems in *atit, matit, vatit*.

Participial Adjectives and Possessives (see Bartholomae, in *K.Z.* xxix. p. 487 seq. = *Flexionslehre* p. 68 seq.— Whitney, *Skt. Gram.* § 441 seq., § 452 seq.)

§ 289. This subdivision of consonant stems includes: —(i) participial (and adjective) stems in *atit;* and (ii) possessive adjective stems in *mant,-vatit*. They are masculine and neuter; the corresponding feminine is made in *a '(ti)tt-*. The stem shows vowel-gradation, strong stem *atit*, weak stem *at* (from *nt;* also GAV. *at*, see § 18 Note).

§ 290. As to stem-gradation, (1) the adjective cistems generally show *at* in the weak (= Skt. weak) cases, (2) the participial (thematic) a-stems show *atit* in almost all forms. (3) The *matit-, v atit*-stems agree with the adjective stems in showing *at* in the weak cases. A number of interchanges, however, between all three occur— these interchanges are found chiefly in YAV. e. g. dat. du. *ber'zanbya* (from str. st.) Ys. 1. 11; 3.13.

i. MASCULINE.

§291. (1) Adjective, Av.-io-"/jj *bar'zatit*-'great' = Skt. *brhdnt*-; (2) Participial, Av. _u *f$uyatit* (c) Derivative Stems in -*is,-us*. § 358. The examples are not numerous. The words are chiefly neuter. There is no vowel-gradation.— Cf. Whitney, *Ski. Gram.* § 414.

§ 363. Comparison of Adjectives. In Avesta as also in Sanskrit, there are two ways of forming the comparative and superlative degrees of adjectives:—(1) -*tara-,-tema*-and (2) -*yah-,-ista*-added to the stem. The corresponding feminine to these is -*tara-,-t3md*-and -*yehi*-(§ 34), -*ista*according to rule, § 362.

(1) -*tara*-(comparative), -*t3ina*-(superlative). § 364. Before -*tara-,-t3ma-*, adjectives whose stern ends in *a* appear commonly in the form *0* as in noun compounds. The o-stems may, however, retain *a* unchanged, as in Sanskrit. Other stems commonly remain unchanged, appearing in the weak form if they have one. *baefazya*-'healing', *bae$azyotara-, bae$azyotama srira*-'fair', *srirotara-,* — *aka*-'bad', *akatara-,* — *huyasta*-'well-sacrificed', *huyastara-,* — *hubao 'di*-'sweet-scented', *hubao 'ditara-, hubao 'diUmaasaojah*-'very strong', *asaojastara-,1 asaojast3-mayaskar't*-'energetic', *yaskarastara-? yaskar'st3tnaamavatit*-'strong', *amavastara-,2 amavastema yaetvah*-'having striven', — *yaetust3ma* (2) -*yak*-(comparative), -*ista*-(superlative). § 365. Before -*yah-,-ista-*, the adjective reverts to its original simple crude stem without formative suffix:

Note 1. Some few adjectives, in appearance at least, show both forms of comparison, as above *aka*-'bad', *akatara-*, and to this also (cf. Note 2) *ajyai-, acilta-;* so superlative *aSaojiSta*-beside *aSaojastara-, afaoyastima*-to *alaojah*-'very strong'.

Note 2. As seen also above, comparatives and superlatives may be more or less mechanically attached to a positive of similar meaning and containing the same crude stem, see § 365: e. g. to *tatyma*-'strong', the comparative *tqijyah-,* superl. *taticUta*-beside' *tamotima-*, et al.

Note 3. The an-stems sometimes follow the analogy of a?/-stems in trteir comparison: e. g. *vir'pravan*-'victorious', comparat. *vir'pravastara-,* superl. *vir'pravastima-;* *aSavan*-'righteous', *a$avastima-;* *vir'prajan*-'victorious', *Vir'prajqstara-, vir'prajqstima.-.* NUMERALS.

§ 366. The numerals in Avesta correspond generally in form and in usage to the Sanskrit equivalents. — Cf. Whitney, *Skt. Gram.* §475 seq.

Av.
100. *sata*-
200. *duye sa 'te*
300. *ti$aro sata*
400. *capwdro sata*
500. *paiica sata*
Av.
600. *fyjivas sata* 700. *hapta sata* 800. *asta sata* 900. *nava sata* 1000. *hazavra*10 000. *baevar*§ 367. The numbers from 11—19, as far as they occur, are made up as in Skt.: e. g. Av. *dvadasa* '12' = Skt. *dvadasa;* Av. *pan.cadasa* '15' = Skt. *pdncadasa*. See below under Ordinals, § 374 b.

Note. Observe, the common forms Av. *prisata*-'30' and *capwar'sata*-'40' arise from transfer of *prisat*-etc. to the a-decl. The strong form *prisatit*-is to be sought in *prisqs* (orig. nom. but crystallized form), etc.

PRONOUNS.

§ 377. Pronominal declension in Avesta agrees in its main outlines with the Sanskrit. A synopsis of the Pronouns in Avesta may be given as follows:— 1. Personal SYNOPSIS
OF
PRONOMINAL-
DECLENSION.

4. Demonstrative

A. Gender not distinguished.

a. First person *azim*. b. Second person *tum*.

I c. Third person, *hi* and other forms.

B. Gender distinguished.

2. Relative — Pronoun *ya*-. 3. Interrogative — Pronoun *ka*-.

(Indefinite.)

a. Demonstrative *ta-(hvd)*. b. Demonstrative *alta*-. c. Demonstrative *alm (a-, »-, ima-, ana-)*. d. Demonstrative *ava-(hau)*.

5. Other pronominal Words and Derivatives.

(Possessive).

(Reflexive).

(Adjectives declined pronominaHy). General Remark. Most of the pronouns in Avesta are closely parallel with those in Sanskrit, and like the latter they show also many marked peculiarities. They are generally made up by combining a number of different stems. The principal points to be observed in regard to their inflection are the following: i—ii. MASCULINE —NEUTER. § 379. Singular:— Nom. Acc. Neut.: Commonly the suffix-/ = Skt.-/ *(d)* — Sometimes in later texts of the YAV. instead of-/, the ending -*m,* like the neuter ending of the noun-declension, is found: e. g. *yim, aom.*

Dat. Abl. Loc.: Show an inserted element -*hm-*= Skt. -*sm-.*—The dat. sg. of the two personal pronouns ends in -*bya (-vya),-byo* = Skt. -*bhya(m),* Whitney, *Skt. Gram.* § 492a.—The loc. sg. in YAV. may take postpositive *a* as in the noun-declension, see § 222. § 380. Plural:—

Nom. (Acc.): The pronominal a-stems make this case end in *e.* This form in *e* often serves also as accusative. Gen.: Shows -*sqm* = Skt. -*sam.*—The 'genitives' *ahmakim, yu$mSkim, ya vakim,* as in Skt., are really crystallized cases nom. acc. neut. of possessives.

Loc.: In YAV. the loc. pl. may take postpositive *a* as in the noundeclension, see § 224. Similarly also in fem. loc. pl. iH. FEMININE.

§ 381. Singular:— Dat. Abl. Gen. Loc. : Show an inserted element -*hy-(-hy-)t-ph-*= Skt. -*sy-.*

§ 382. Plural:— Gen.: Shows -*vhqm* = Skt. -*sam.*

§ 383. Interchange of Neuter with Feminine Forms.

As in the nouns § 232, so also in the pronouns the neuter plural often assumes the form of the feminine or rather interchanges with it.—See also Johannes Schmidt, *Pluralbildungen der indogerm. Neutra* pp. 21, 260, etc.

Note. In formulaic passages, especially in the Yashts (e. g. Yt. 5-13,15), masc. forms *yeyhe, a'pfte, ahmSi* are sometimes used instead of the proper fem. forms. This arises from the mosaic character of such passages.

§ 384. General Relative Case is found in YAV. in the instances of *ydis* as plural, cf. § 229.—For the treatment of *yd, yaf, yim* as stereotyped case (plural and singular) see under Syntax.

A. GENDER NOT DISTINGUISHED, i. Personal Pronouns.

§ 385. The first and second personal pronouns, as in Skt., show many peculiarities and individulities of inflection. Some cases also use two forms, a fuller and a briefer form, according to the position of the pronoun in

§ 390. (b) Second Person, Av. *for tum* 'thou' = Skt.

§ 394. (c) Third Person, Av. (up) *he ($e)* and other forms.

The proper third personal pronoun *htm, he* etc. (enclitic) is defective; its deficiencies are partly supplied by the demonstrative pronoun, and partly by enclitic forms of *di-, i-*used with personal force. These latter show distinction of gender, but they may best be included here.

§ 395-The following forms of the proper third personal (often used anaphorically, sometimes used reflexively, see also §416) occur in GYAV.; they are all enclitic:

Singular. Acc. *him* (GYAV.); Dat. Gen. *hi* or *$e%* 155 (YAV.), *hoi* (GAV. ). — Dual. N.A.V. *hi* (GAV.). — Plural. Acc. *hil* (GYAV.). Note 1. The form *hi* dat. gen. sg. seems in some passages in YAV. to serve as plural. See under Syntax.

Note 2. With the above Avesta forms compare Skt. acc. sg. *sim;* Prakrit dat. gen. *si* — all enclitic. See Wackernagel in *A".Z.* xxiv. p. 605 seq.

§ 396. Similar to *he* in usage are the forms from stem YAV. *di-* likewise enclitic:—

Sg. Acc. *dim* m. f.; *di(* n. — PI. Acc. *diS* m. f.; *din.* Ys. 65.8.

§ 397-Of like usage (cf. also § 422), is stem G(Y)Av. *i-*enclitic—sometimes employed almost pleonastically:—

Sg. Acc. *im* m.; *»/* n. (GAV.), # (YAV., particle). — Du. N.A.V. *i.* — PI. Nom. *i* n.; Acc. *»/* m.; *i* n.

§ 398. On *hvd, hvavya* used as personal (and reflexive) see §§ 416, 436 Note 3.

B. GENDER DISTINGUISHED.
2. Relative Pronoun.

§ 399. Relative Av.-«fo *ya-*'who, which' = Skt. *yd-.*

The relative stem *ya-, yd-*= Skt. *yd-, yd-,* shows the following forms.—Cf. Whitney, *Skt. Gram.* § 508.

3. Interrogative Pronoun. § 406. Interrogative Av. *ka-*'who, which, what?' = Skt. *kd-.*

The interrogative *ka-, kd-*= Skt. *kd-, kd-,* is identical in inflection with the relative and requires no full paradigm to be given.—Cf. Whitney, *Skt. Gram.* § 504.

i. MASCUUNE — NEUTER.

Note. YAV. also an instr. sg. *kana* = Skt. *kina* beside Av. *ka.*— YAV. also dat. *cahmSi* (indef.) beside *kahmSi;* GAV. *cahya* beside *kahyS.* —YAV. as gen. pl. (or perhaps fem. sg. form = neut.) *kqm* m. f.

§ 407. Some special forms of interrogative are worthy of note.

1) Stem *ki-, ci-*'quis':—Sg. Nom. (m. f. ) *ciS/* cf. Skt. *nd-kis;* Acc. (m. n.) *dm, eim,* cf. Skt. *kim.* — PI. Nom. (m. n.) *kaya, cayo.* — *Heut.* also Sg. Nom. Acc. *ci(, ct(.* 2) Stem *kati-, cati-*'what, how much': — Sg. Acc. (neut.) *ca'ti* = Skt. *kdti.*

Note. Here also Av. *etna-*'what'.— Likewise some forms of the interrogative used adverbially: — e. g. *ka(* 'how, nonne?'. — *ctl* 'how'. Perhaps *kim* Vd. 17.1 (?). — Uncertain *cyavha(* 'how' Ys. 44.12 abl. (?) or *ci-avha(* doubtful.

Indefinite.

§ 408. The indefinite force is usually given in Av., as in Skt., by combining a particle -*cif, -«/*=Skt. -*cit,-ca,-caf* etc., with the interrogative or relative. Sometimes it is added by the particle -*cina -cana* Afr. 3.7 = Skt. -*cand),* which is likewise attached to nouns and adjectives; sometimes, again, reduplication of the pronoun (rel. interrog.) gives an indefinite or a distributive force.

Av. *kahmdicif* 'to whomsoever' = Skt. *kdsmdicit;* Av. *kajacina* 'howsoever, in any way'; *cayascd* 'qui 4. Demonstrative Pronouns.

§ 409. (a) Demonstrative Av. *ta-* 'this' = Skt. *td-.*

The demonstrative stem Aa-, ha-, ta-'6, Yi, To' = Skt. ja-, ja-, serves also as personal of the third person.— Cf. Whitney, *Skt. Gram.* § 495.

i. MASCULINE—NEUTER.

§ 417. (b) Demonstrative Av. -*"r"* aeta-'this' = Skt. *etd-.*

The demonstrative *ae$a-, ae$d-, aeta-*'this, here' = Skt. *ifd-, e$d-, etd-,* is identical in declension with ha-, ha-, *ta*from which it is derived by prefixing *ae*-which makes it the nearer demonstrative. The only GAV. form noted is

Forms to be observed in GAV. and YAV.

i. MASCULINE —NEUTER. § 418. Singular:— Nom.: YAV. also *al$a* = Skt. *ltd*, Whitney, *Skt. Gram.* § 176a, cf. *ha* above § 411. § 419. Plural:—
Nom. Acc.: YAV. notice that *alte* like *te* above §§413, 380 serves as both nom. and acc. masc. and also neut.

ii. NEUTER.

§ 420. Plural: — Nom. Acc.: YAV. also (like fem., § 383) *atm*.—On *alte* see § 380. Gen.: YAV. also (contaminated with fem.) *altavkqm*.

Hi. FEMININE.

§ 421. Singular:— Nom.: GAV. (only occurrence) *al$a* Ys. 12.9.

Gen.: YAV. the form *altaya, altayms-ci(* follows the noun-inflection, 3-decl.

§ 422. (c) Demonstrative Av. *aim* 'this' = Skt. *ay dm.*

The demonstrative *aim*, as in Skt., is made up from defective stems *a-, i-, ima-, ana-*= Skt. *a-, i-, ima-, ana*combined to fill out a complete declension.

It is to be observed (in GAV. it is evident) that beside the accented forms, there occur likewise unaccented forms (not found at beginning of a pada). These forms generally come from the brief stem.

Forms to be observed in GAV. and TAV.

§ 423. GAV. has in general the same forms as YAV., with lengthened final wherever possible. There are also some peculiarities worthy of note.

i. MASCULINE —NEUTER. § 424. Singular:— Nom.: GAV. also *aySm* beside *alm*, see § 32. Abl.: YAV. also *akmS(*, on *S* see § 19(b). Gen.: GAV. *ahyS, ayS-ca*, cf. §§ 132, 133. Loc.: YAV. also (with postpos. *a*, § 379) *ahmya*.

§ 432. (d) Demonstrative *hdu, ava-* 'that' = Skt. *asdii,* —.

The remote demonstrative in Av. *ava-*'that, yonder' (cf. Old Pers. *ava-*), combined with *hdu*, is to be contrasted with Skt. *attiu-, asdii-.* The Av. shows *di)a*throughout where the Skt. has *amu-* .—Cf. Whitney, *Skt. Gram.* § 501.

5. Other Pronominal Words and Derivatives. Possessive — Reflexive, Pronom-

inal Derivatives and Adverbs.

§ 434. Under the above head belong the possessives and a number of words which have chiefly the nature of adjectives and are inflected partly according to the pronominal declension, partly according to the nominal. They answer in general to corresponding forms in Sanskrit.— Cf. Whitney, *Skt. Gram.* § 515 seq.

Possessive —Reflexive. § 435. Here may be enumerated as connected with the personal pronoun, the following possessive (and reflexive) forms: — Av. *ma-*'meus', *pwa-*'tuus', *hva-, ha-, hava-*(reflexive) 'suus', *ahmdka-*'our', *yu$mdka-, fy$mdka*'your'.—*mavatit-*'like me', *pwdvaut-*'like thee', *yupnd-vatit-, fy$mdvatit-*'like you'.—*hraepalpya-*'own'.

Other Pronominal Derivatives and Adverbs.

§ 436. The following derivatives may further be noted:—Relative, *yavatit-*'how much', *yatdra-*'which of two'. — Interrogative, *cvatit-*'how much?', *katdra-*'which of two?'.—Demonstrative, *aetavatit-*'so much', *avatt-*'that, such', *avavatit-(avatit-*§ 194) 'so much'.—Likewise here, numerous pronominal adverbs *ya-pa* 'how, as', *ka-da* 'how, when?', *cu* 'how?', *i-da* 'here', etc.

Note 1. Here observe Av. *hatd* 'reciprocally, each other' = Skt. *svdtas.*

Note 2. On *hvd* 'ipse, ille' as personal pronoun, see §§ 398, 416.

Note 3. From same stem as *hvd* (in Note 2) comes the interesting reflex, dat. *hvavoya* 'self (like *mSvya* § 388), cf. Lat. *s(v)ibi.*

Note 4. From an assumed demonstrative stem *tva-*comes the neut. adverb *pwa(* 'then again' Ys. 44.3 = Skt. *tvat.*

Note 5. Instances of GAV. *ahya* gen. of demonstr. (= pers.), from *alm* § 422, instead of the reflex, possessive, occur.

Declension of Pronominal Derivatives.

§ 437. In regard to inflection, the pronominal derivatives follow partly the pronominal declension and partly the nominal. The following forms of the possessives (reflexive), and of the demonstrative derivatives declined according to the pronominal declension

are worthy of note.

Adjectives declined pronominally. § 443. A few adjectives in Av., like their corresponding Skt. equivalents, also follow the pronominal declension wholly or in part. Cf. Whitney, *Skt. Gram.* §522 seq.— Instances are: Av. *aeva-*'one, alone'; Av. *any a-*'other' = Skt. *anyd-;* Av, *vis/a-*'all' = Skt. *visva-.*

For example: Pl. Nom. Acc. m. *vispe, vispi* (pronominal) beside Nom. m. *vtspavho;* Acc. *vtspSs-ca* (YAV.), *vis-pqs-cS, vtspitig* (GAV.) i. e. nominal declension; — Gen. *vispal$qm* (pronominal) beside *vtspanqm* (nominal); et al.

CONJUGATION, VERBS.

§ 444. The Avesta verb corresponds closely to the Sanskrit in form, character, and in usage. The Av. texts, however, are not so extensive as to give the verb complete in all its parts; some few gaps in the conjugationsystem therefore occur.

Modelled after the Sanskrit, the Avesta verbal system may be presented as on the next page.

§ 445. Voice, Mode, Tense. The Av. agrees with the Skt. — especially with the language of the Vedas — in voices active, middle (passive), in tenses present (and preterite), perfect (and pluperfect), aorist, future, and in modes indicative, imperative, subjunctive, optative. In usage likewise these generally correspond with the Sanskrit.

Note 1. The middle voice, as in Skt., is often used with a passive force. A formative passive, as in Skt., however also occurs (cf. V. a).

Note 2. Under tenses, observe that 'injunctive' or 'improper subjunctive' is a convenient designation for certain forms of augmentless preterites used with imperative force. These are enumerated under the simple preterite. Cf. Whitney, *Skt. Gram.* § 563.

§ 446. Infinitive, Participle. Like the Skt., the Av. conjugation-system possesses also infinitive forms (abstract verbal nouns) and participial forms (active and middle in each tense-system) and gerundives. See VI below.

§ 447. Person, Number. The Av. like the Skt. distinguishes three persons, and three numbers.

Note. It is to be observed that the first persons imperat. are supplied by subjunctive forms-.

SYNOPSIS
OF
VERB-
SYSTEM

I. Present-System d (10 Classes) II. Perfect-System III. Aorist-System d J (non-J-, and j-Class) d a. Perfect . (Present).
1. Indicative b. Pluperfect (Preterite). 2. Imperative. 3. Subjunctive (Pres. and Pret. F6rms). 4. Optative. (5. Participle.
1. Indicative (Preterite = Aor.). 2. Imperative. 3. Subjunctive (Pres. and Pret. Forms). 4. Optative. 5. Participle. IV. Future-System x-Indi
I 2. Pari
Indicative (A c t. and M i d.).
Participle. .
V. Secondary Conjugations.
a. Passive. d. Inchoative. b. Causative. e. Desiderative. c. Denominative. f. Intensive. VI. Verbal Abstract Forms. a. Participles, b. Gerunds, c. Infinitives. IVII. Periphrastic Verbal Phrases.
§ 448. Personal Endings. These are either (a) primary (pres. and fut. indie, and partly subjunct.) or they are (b) secondary (pret. indie, opt, aor., and partly subjunct.). Some individual peculiarities of form occur in (c) the imperative and in (d) the perfect; the endings, therefore, of the latter two also are separately enumerated.
The scheme of normal endings in comparison with the Skt,—cf. Whitney, *Skt. Gratn.* § 553—is as follows: (Observe the Av. 3 du. forms often identical with Skt. 2 du.) a. Primary Endings.
i. ACTIVE. U. MIDDLE.
Av. Singular: cf. Skt. Av. Singular: cf. Skt.
1. -*mi mi-e e* 2. -*hi (-?i)..-si (-si)-(w)ke (-$e)...-si (-fi) $.-ti....-u-te te*
Dual: Dual: *li-vahi* (GAV.) -*vas* — *vahi* 2. *thas* — -*athi* 3. -*to,-pd..-tas-ape-an*
Plural: Plural: 1. -*mahi...-masi* (Ved.) -*ma'de make* 2. -*pa* .... -*tha-pwe dhve* 3- -*flti nti-nte nil* b. Secondary Endings.
i. ACT1YE. ii. MIDDLE.
Av. Singular: cf. Skt. Av. Singular: cf. Skt.
1. -*in-m-i,-a i,-a* 2. -*s (-s) s (-s)-vha (-fa)... -that* 3.-/ / -*ta ta*

Dual: Dual: 1. -*Va-va* — -*vahi* 2. — -*tam* —-*athatn* 3. -*t3in* .... -*iSm-atem-atom*

General Remarks on the Endings.

§ 449. In general, GAV. has the same forms as YAV. above, with the long final vowel wherever possible, cf. § 26; but there are also a number of peculiarities to be remarked upon in connection with GAV. as well as with reference to YAV.
1 Sporadic, cf. § 457. b. Secondary Endings (Observations). § 453. Singular:—
First Person: ii. MIDDLE. Observe that the normal ending *i* coalesces with the final of an a-stem into -*e:* e. g. *aguze* 'I hid myself opp.
to *aoji* 'I spake'.—The ending -*a* is found in the optative. Second Person: i. ACTIVE. The normal ending -*s* unites with *a* in the a-conj. and gives -*o* (-# subjunct.); the /-form occurs according to rule § 156.—ii. MIDDLE. VGA v. notice the suffix is -*sa* (cf. Gk.-00) contrasted with Skt. -*thas.* Third Person: i. ACTIVE. YGAV., orig. *t* is retained (unchanged to-/) after J *(J),* e.g. *moist* 'he turned', *coUt* 'he promised', §§ 81, 192. —Notice *Ss* (i. e. *Ss-t)* 'he was' and *cinas* 'he promised' § 192 Note. § 454-Dual:—
Third Person: i. ACTIVE. YAV., observe that the 3 du. Av. -*tim* is in form like the 2 du. Skt. -*tam—on* this interchange in form between 3 du. and 2 du. see § 449 Note.—ii. MIDDLE. YGAV. , note Av. -*atim* opp. to Skt. -*atom,* see again § 449 Note.—Again (like primary 2 du., but) with secondary meaning YAV. -*bVpe* — Skt. -*athi* and some other forms—see Bartholomae, *K.Z.* xxix. p. 286 seq. = *Flexionslehre* p. 17 seq.
§ 455. Plural:—
First Person: ii. MIDDLE. Observe that GAV. has a proper secondary ending -*ma'di* (cf. opt. *va'rima'di)* = Skt. -*mahi,* but YAV. substitutes for this -*ma'de* drawn from the present.
Second Person: ii. MIDDLE. GAV. shows -*dam* = Skt. -*dhvam,* § 63.
Third Person: i. ACTIVE. In redupl. formations GAV. has occasionally an unthematic 3 pl. pret. in -*a(* (i. e. -*nt)* corresponding to the occasional -*ati* =-*nti* of the pres., e. g. *zaza(* 'they drove away', et al. —GYAV., remark also opt. -

*Sr'I,-Sr',* thus *buyar'S* 'they would be', *hyar'* beside *hyqn.* Also -*ar'* aor. pret. GAV. *Sdar'* 'they made' Ys. 43.15 = Skt. *adur;* YAV. *aMar'* 'they elapsed' Vd. 1. 4, cf. Whitney, *Skt. Gram.* §§ 829, 550 — cf. also under perfect endings (Pf. ii, below). —ii. MIDDLE. YAV. also sporadic traces of secondary 3 pl. mid. -*rim* = Skt. -*ram* in Av. *vaozirim* Yt. 19.69, cf. Whitney, *Skt. Gram.* § 834 b (perhaps best as pluperf.).
c. Imperative Endings (Observations). § 456. Singular:—
Second Person: i. ACTIVE. YGAV., the a-verbs (thematic) have no ending, the simple stem form in -*a,-a* is used.—The non-a-verbs (unthematic) show -*di* (-*di* § 83, 1), GAV. -*dt.*—ii. MIDDLE. YAV. regularly -*vuha* = Skt. -*sva* —GAV. -*sva* (in *dasvS* 'give' = *dad-sva* § 186), -*M,-ftvS* § 130, 2 a. Third Person: ii. MIDDLE. A suffix -*qm* = Skt. -*Sm,* 3 sg. mid. is found in GAV. *ir'iucqm* 'let him speak aright' Ys. 48.9, *vidqm* 'shall decide' *vi-j-dS* Ys; 32.6, Geldner, in *B.B.* xv. p. 261, cf. Whitney, *5/. Gram.* § 618. § 457-Plural:
Second Person: i. ACTIVE—ii. MIDDLE. The forms are undistinguishable from an augmentless imperfect § 445 Note 2.—A genuine instance of -*na* cf. Skt. -*tana* 2 pl. active imperat. is GAV. *bar anS* Ys. 30.9, cf. Skt. *bhajatana,* Whitney, *Skt. Gram.* § 740.
Third Person: i. ACTIVE—ii. MIDDLE. The endings -*atitu,-stitu,-ititqm* occur in both a-verbs and in non-a-verbs — (in the latter case by transfer § 471 to a-conj.).
d. Perfect Endings. § 458. For observations on the perfect endings see Pf. ii below.

Mode-Formation.
1. Indicative Mode.
§ 459. The indicative has no special mode-sign other than the use of the present stem itself. The endings are the primary in the present, the secondary in the preterite.
Note. For special remarks on the strong and weak stem-forms in the indicative, see below §§ 467, 476 and observe under the different conjugation classes.
2. Imperative Mode. (Cf. Whitney, *Skt.*

*Gram.* § 569.)

§ 460. The imperative has no characteristic modesign, the stem is identical with that of the indicative, the special endings are simply added.

Note 1. For special remarks on the strong and weak stem-forms see below under the imperatives of the various conjugation-classes. Note 2. For remarks on the endings see § 456.

3. Subjunctive Mode. (Cf. Whitney, *Skt. Gram.* § 557 seq.)

§ 461. In Av., as in Skt., the subjunctive has as its characteristic mark an *a* added to the stem to form the special mode-stem. In the a-conjugation (thematic) this *a* unites of course with the stem-final and forms *d*:—e. g. (i) thematic a-stem, Av. *bara-hi* 'mayest thou bear' (i. e. *bara-a-hi*) = Skt. *bhdr-d-si;* '—) un-thematic, Av. *jan-aMi* 'may he smite' (cf. pres. indicat. *ja'tirti*) = Skt. *hdn-a-ti.*

§ 462. The endings of the subjunctive are partly primary (i. e. pres. subjunct. ), partly secondary (i.e. pret. subjunct.). — the former predominating. Observe in 1 sg. active YGAV.-«/,-«» (i. e. *-Sni*) or also YGAV. *-a,-S;*—and in 1 sg. middle it is *-ne* (i.e. *-ane*) beside *-Si.* Cf. Whitney, *Skt. Gram.* § 562.

Subjunctive Endings combined with Mode-Sign.

i. ACTIVE. Av. Singular: 1. *-ant,-a.... (Shi).. -a -a'ti* 11. MIDDLE.

Note 1. Observe (late) YAV. 2 sg. *-Si* = *-Shi* § 450.

Note 2. On improper subjunctive or imperative see § 445 Note 2.

4. Optative Mode. (Cf. Whitney, 5£f. *Gram.* § 564 seq.)

§ 463. The characteristic mode-sign of the optative in Av., as in Skt., is *-yd-,-i*-added to the weak-stem for the non-a-conjugation (unthematic), or it is *-I*-added to the regular tense-stem of the class for the a-conjugation (thematic).

In the a-stems (thematic) the mode-sign *-i*-unites with the stem-final *a* into *-ae-(-oi-)* §§ 55, 56. In the nono-conj. the distinction between *-yd-,-i*-is that *-yd*-was employed in the active and *-I*-in the middle.

Note. Instead of instances of *-t-*(§21 Note) occur, e. g. *daipiia* beside *da'diia*

'mayest thou give'.— Similarly occur instances of *-yS*-for *-yS*-(§ 18 Note 1), cf. *buyata, buyama* 'may ye, we be'.— Probably also GAV. *da'dya(* Ys. 44.10.

§ 464. The endings of the optative are the secondary ones throughout. In YAV. , however, the 1 pl. mid. *-ma'de* (primary, e. g. Ys. 9.21) instead of GAV. -*ma'di* (secondary) is found. Observe in the o-conj. (thematic) the 3 pl. act. mid. Av. *-in,-snta* (cf. Gk. Xif-ot-ev, Xey-oi-VTo) is to be contrasted with Av. non-a-verbs which show *-ar',-ar'S* = Skt. -*ur;-ran* (act. mid. in both *a*-and non-a-stems).

Optative Endings combined with Mode-Sign.

a. a-conjugation (thematic).

i. ACTIVE. ii. MIDDLE.

Reduplication and Augment.

a. Reduplication. (Cf. Whitney, *Skt. Gram.* § 588 seq.)

§ 465. (a) Reduplication in Av., as in Skt., is found in certain parts of the verb-conjugation (pres. of 3rd. class, and in the desiderative, and intensive), in the perfect, and sometimes in the aorist. The reduplication consists in the repetition of a part of the root.—The rules of reduplication should be noted:— (b) A long internal or final vowel of the root is commonly shortened in the reduplicated syllable; sometimes —see desiderative, intensive—it is lengthened or strengthened. Radical *ar* (r-vowel) is reduplicated by *i.* An initial vowel, by repetition of itself, of course merely becomes long in reduplicating.

(c) Roots beginning with a consonant repeat that consonant, but a guttural is reduplicated by the corresponding palatal; an original *s* (including *st, sp, sm*) is reduplicated by *h,* an orig. palatal *s* by *s,* an initial spirant by the corresponding smooth:—e.g. *Kv. ja-jm-af* (√gam-'go'), *hi-sta-'tiystd*-'stand'), *ki-spds-3mna* (√*spas*'see'), *hi-smar-3nto* (√*mar-, smar*-'remember'), *tu-pru-ye* (√*pru*-'nourish').

Note 1. The original guttural instead of palatal is retained in reduplication before *u,* cf. Av. *ku-nv-qna* (√fi$nu*-'rejoice, please').

Note 2. Observe the redupl. form (desiderative participle) *zi-niBvhimna*

Yt. 13.49, cf. Skt. *ji-jftSs-amanas.* b. Augment.

(Cf. Whitney, *Skt. Gram.* § 585.)

§ 466. In Av. the augment is comparatively rare, the instances of its omission far exceed in proportion those of the Vedic Sanskrit.

The augment, as in Skt., consists of short *a* prefixed to the preterite tense—imperfect, aorist, pluperfect. This *a,* as likewise in Skt, combines with an initial vowel into the corresponding *vrddki.*

It is often difficult to decide whether an *a* is the augment *a* or the verbalprefix *a* = *d.*

Note 1. For metrical purposes it seems sometimes that augment must be restored in reading where the texts omit it. — See Geldner, *Metrik* p. 38.

Note 2. Instead of *a,* GAV. shows once a form *i* in augment before *v,* cf. GAV. *Ivaoca(* (but written . *voacaf)* § 32.

Note 3. On augmentless preterites ('injunctive') with imperat.subjunct. force, see § 445 Note.

§ 467. Vowel-Variation (Strong and Weak). In Av., quite as in Skt., verb-stems commonly show vowel-variation —strongest, middle or strong, and weak forms, cf. § 235. This phenomenon must of course go hand in hand with an original shift of accent.

I. PRESENT-SYSTEM.

§468. The present-system is the most important of the systems, its forms are by far the most frequent in occurrence, and upon the basis of present-formation may be founded in Av., as in Skt., the conjugation-groups and classification of verbs. See the following § 469.

Classes of Verbs.

§ 469. Taking the Sanskrit Grammar as model, we may in the Av. present-system likewise distinguish ten classes of verbs according to the method of forming the present-stem. In Av., however, the phenomenon of accent (§ 2 end) is not always so clearly discernible.

The ten classes fall into two great groups of conjugation according as the endings are attached to the root with or without the (thematic) stem-vowel *a.* The (I) first group, the thematic or a-conjugation (CI. 1,6,4, IO), assumes *a* in the formation of its present-stem; the (II) second group, the unthematic or non-a-conjugation (CI. 2, 3, 7, 5, 8, 9), attaches the endings directly to the root (the latter as stem, however, subject to modification) without this *a* as formative element of the stem.—Cf.Whitney, *Skt. Gram.* § 602 seq.

§ 470. The classification of Av. verbs on the basis of the Sanskrit Grammar is the following: — I. -Conjugation (thematic).
First Formation—Class 1—see § 478 seq.
(1) a-class with strengthened root-form = Skt. first *(bhti-)* class.
Av. *fba-, bav-a-'ti* 'he becomes'.
Second Formation—Class 6—see § 479 seq. (6) o-class with unstrengthened root-form = Skt. sixth *(tud-)* class.
Av. *fdruj-, drui-ati* 'he deceives'.
Third Formation—Class 4—see § 480 seq. (4) ja-class (unstrengthened root-form) = Skt. fourth *(div-)* class.
Av. *fnas-, nas-ye-'ti* 'he vanishes'.
Fourth Formation—Class 10—see § 481 seq. (10) ya-class (strengthened root-form), causal = Skt. tenth *(cur-)* class.
Av. *fruc-, raoc-aye-'ti* 'he lights up'.
II. Non-a-Conjugation (unthematic).
First Formation—Class 2—see § 516 seq.
(2) Root-class—root itself is present stem = Skt. second *(ad-)* class.
Av. *fjan-,* 'he smites'.
Second Formation—Class 3—see § 540 seq.
(3) Reduplicating class—root redupl. is pres. stem =
Skt. third *(hu-)* class.
Av. *fda-, da-dS-'ti* 'he gives'.
Third Formation—Class 7—see § 554 seq.
(7) Nasal-class—inserted -na-(str.), -n- (wk.) = Skt. seventh *(rudh-)* class.
Av. *fric-, 'ri-na-fiti* 'lets go'.
Fourth Formation—Class 5—see § 566 seq. (5) «#-class—root adds *nao-* (str.), *nu-*(wk.) = Skt. fifth *(su-)* class.
Av. *fkar-, kir'-nao-'ti* 'he makes'.
Fifth Formation—Class 8—see § 577 seq.
(8) «-class—root adds «-alone = Skt. eigth *(tan-)* class.

Av. *fap-, Sfitite* (i. e. *ap-v-ante* § 95) 'are overtaken'.
Sixth Formation—Class 9—see § 584 seq.
(9) «a-class—root adds *na-*(str.), *n-, na-* (wk.) = Skt. ninth *(kri-)* class.
Av. *fgarw-, gar'w-na-'ti* 'he seizes'.
§ 471. Transfer of Conjugation. A verb is not always inflected according to one and the same conjugation and class throughout. The majority of the forms of a verb may be made up after one conjugation and class of the present system, while a few forms of the same verb may be made up after another; the same part of the verb being thus occasionally formed according to two classes. Instances of such transition in forms from one class to another are not rare; in general, examples of the tendency for verbs of the non-a-conjugation (unthematic) to pass over to the inflection of the a-conjugation, are not difficult to find.—See §§ 529, 553 etc.
i. The -Conjugation (thematic).
§ 472. General Remark. The thematic or a-conjugation in the present-system comprises four classes (CI. 1, 6, 4, 10), in all which the endings are attached to the root by means of a thematic vowel *a* (in 1 person *a, a).* The root-vowel may, or may not be strengthened according to the class of the verb; it remains then as in the indicative throughout the other modes of the presentsystem.—The verbs of the a-conj. are numerous.—Cf. Whitney, *Skt. Gram.* § 733 seq.
Note. The 1 plur. thematic shows *S* more often than *a* (Skt. *a): e. g. Av. yazSma 'de* commoner than *barSma 'de.*
Mode Formation—Special Remark.
1. Indicative.
§ 473. The various endings are simply attached by means of the thematic *a* (in 1 person *a)* directly to the stem formed according to the rules of its particular class.
2. Imperative.
§ 474. The normal endings are attached by means of the thematic *a* directly to the present-stem of the class. 3. Subjunctive.
§ 475. The characteristic *a* of the subjunctive unites with the thematic *a* into

*a* in attaching the subjunctive endings given above, § 462.
4. Optative.
§ 476. In the fl-verbs the optative sign is *-i-*(instead of *-yd-*) and it unites with the thematic *a* into *-ae-*(-? § 56) in attaching the endings.
5. Participle.
§ 477. The participial forms (verbal adjectives) are made in each class by attaching to the present-stem the formative element *-tit* (§ 291, *-n.ti* fem.) for the active, and *-mna* (§ 237, *-mna* fem. )—also *-ana (-ana),* see Note—for the middle.
Note. On middle ptcpl. in *-Sna (-ana)* see § 507.
Classes of the a-Conjugation (thematic).
CI. 1, 6, 4, 10.
§ 478. Class 1—a-class with strengthened rootform = Skt. first *(bhii-)* class.—To form the present-stem,
Forms to be observed in GAV. and YAV.
§ 489. GAV. shows in general the same forms as above, but with the long final vowel, cf. § 26. It has, however, a certain number of individual differences; these as well as other variations in YAV. also may here be noted.
§ 490. (1) The original unmodified forms of 3 pl. act. mid. *-atiti,-atite,* cf. *zava 'tite* above, occasionally stand instead of being changed to *-gfyti,-atite,* e. g.:— GAV. *vana 'titt,* YAV. *va.nan.ti* 'they win' Yt. 13.154, GAV. *haca 'tite* beside YAV. *hacitite* 'they follow' (§§ 30, 491).
§ 491. (2) According to § 30, the forms *-ititi,-itite,-in* are often found after palatals, instead of *-atiti,-a 'fiti* etc., e. g.:—
Av. *fratacinti* 'they run forth' (variants *"taca 'titi, "taotiti* Ys. 65.3, *ytac-), fratacin* 'they ran forth'; *hacitite* (YAV.) beside *haca 'tite* 5. Participle.
§ 506. On the relation of Av. *-mna* (metrically often *-mana)* to Skt. *-mSna,* see § 18 Note 2.
§ 507. In Av. more often than in Skt. (cf. Whitney, *Skt. Gram.* § 741 a) there appear instances of middle (passive) participles of a-verbs formed with the participial suffix *-ana,-ana* (= Skt. *-Sna,* § 18) instead of *-mna,* e.g. *barana-*

'bearing', *"azana* 'driving';—*yazSna*-'worshipping'; *starana-*'strewing'.

ii. The non-«-Conjugation (unthematic).

§ 508. General Remark. In Av., as in Skt., the verbs of the non-tf-conjugation (unthematic) are not so numerous as those of the thematic conjugation. They may be grouped in six classes (CI. 2, 3, 7, 5, 8, 9), in each of which the endings are attached directly (without an interposed *a)* to the stem which is subject to modification.

The striking characteristic of the entire group is the variation of the root in different forms. The modified root or the suffix assumes now a stronger form, again a weaker form.

§ 509. Strong and Weak Stem-Forms. The strong *(guna)* forms, as a rule, are:—(1) the Sing. Indic. Act. (Pres. Pret.),—(2) the 3rd. Sing. Imperat. Act. ,—(3) the entire Subjunct.—The remaining forms are weak. Many fluctuations and transfers, however, occur; especially often is the strong stem employed in forms (see 3rd. plurals) modelled after the a-conjugation.

Mode Formation.—Special Remark.
1. Indicative.

§ 510. The endings of the non-thematic indicative require some remark. GAV. generally shows the older use of -*mi* (§ 450) and -*a 'ti,-a 'te,-af* (for thematic -*atiti,-an.te-an* § 452). In YAV. this old distinction is not sharply preserved. The stem in general to which the endings are directly attached shows a variation of str. and wk. forms according to the preceding rule, § 509.

2. Imperative. § 511. The ending of the Imperat. 2 sing, is -*di,-di.* The endings in general are attached directly to the prepared class-stem. This shows the strong form in the 3 sg. act.; in the other forms it has the weak grade, but fluctuations occur. 3. Subjunctive. § 512. The endings are attached by means of the mode-sign *a* to the prepared class-stem which shows the strong form throughout. 4. Optative.

§ 513. The regular optative endings are attached by the mode-sign -*yd-,-i-(1)* in accordance with the rules given above at § 463. The stem regularly shows its weak form throughout, but variations

from this sometimes occur.
5. Participle.

§ 514. The participial forms (verbal adjectives) are made by attaching to the present stem in its weak grade the formative element -*atit,-af* (i. e. -*nt)* for the active, and -*ana,-ana* beside -*mna,* for the middle.

Classes of the non-a-Conjugation (unthematic). CI. 2, 3. 7. 5. 8, 9. § 515. The six classes of unthematic verbs have certain characteristics in common but they have also certain individual peculiarities, these classes will now each be taken up in detail.

Class 2—Root-Class. § 516. Class 2—Root-Class—root itself is present stem = Skt. second *(ad-)* class.—The stem may have the strong or the weak form according to § 509, the endings

Forms to be observed in GAV. and YAV. § 524. Beside the above paradigm, a certain number of forms in GAV. and YAV. are worthy of note.

I. Indicative,
a. Present.

§ 525. Singular:— First Person: i. ACTIVE. GAV., notice (from strongest stem) *stSumi* 'I praise' (but v. 1. *staomi*) Ys. 43.8, cf. Skt. *sISuti* (Ved. 3 sg.). Second Person: i. ACTIVE. YAV., observe likewise as regular form (§ 122) *pahi* 'thou protectest'. Third Person: ii. MIDDLE. YAV. also (like 1st.—3rd. sg. pres., above) *ni-jne* 'he smites'.

1 Yt. 5.82. — 8 a-conj. cf. §§ 486, 452 end. — Cf. § 21 Note. — 4 Cf. Skt. *std-vana-,* Whitney § 619d. — 6 i.e. like a-conj. ptcpl.

Forms to be observed.

§ 537-YAV., notice in a late passage Yt. 34.12 (2 pl. opt. with primary ending I) *h-yi-pa* 'might ye be'.

§ 538. Transfers to the s-conjugation:— 1. Indic. Pret. 3 sg. *avh-a-(.*—3. Subjunct. 3 sg. *avhS- 'ti.*

§ 539. Beside all the above paradigm of the present-system, there is made from this root *ah* 'to be', as in Skt., a regular perfect *Onha* etc. § 606 = Skt. *dsa* etc.

1. Indicative. i. ACT. a. Pres. YAV. *dap-a- 'ti, da-i-titi.*— b. Pret. YGAV. *dap-i-m, dap-d, dap-a-(, dad-a-(; dap-i-n, dad-i-n* (beside *dada(* § 543 Foot-Note).—

ii. MID. YAV. *dap-a-Uc*— GAV. *dad-i-tite* 'they are placed'. Note. Similarly transferred A v. *zizanititi, zizamn, zizani(* from *fzan-*'beget, bear'. The Skt. shows *jijanat* as redupl. a or. Whitney, *Skt. Gram.* § 864.

Class 7.—Nasal Class.

§ 554. The roots of the nasal class all end in a consonant; the class has for its characteristic feature the assumption of an internal nasal to form the stem. That is, the root has a -*na*-(in strong forms), an -*n*-(in weak forms) inserted immediately before its final consonant to form the present stem. The root itself retains its weak grade; the endings are attached directly to the stem.— Cf. Skt. seventh Class, Whitney, *Skt. Gram.* § 683 seq.

Here belong for example: Av. *yds-*'to announce, promise' *ci-na-sti;* Av. *y 'ric-*'to let go' *'ri-na-ti*=Skt. *ri-na-kti,* and some others—see following paradigm §555. Paradigm of Class 7. (Cf. Whitney, *Skt. Gram.* § 684.) § 555-Av. *fciS-*'to announce, promise', *Hp-*'to proclaim, think', *mark-(msr 'tic-)* 'kill', *kart-*'to cut', *mis-*'mingle', *vid-*'find, receive'. Cf. Skt. y*chid-*'to cut'.

§ 556. 1. Indicative.—a. Present.
ii. MIDDLE.
Av. Singular: cf. Skt.
*par '-na-ne* — i., _-. *fn-nai prt-pSi* 3.
*par '-na-He pri-vd-tSi*
Plural:, 3. *v3r '-nm-tite1 vr-vd-ntii*

§ 589. 5. Participle.
ii. Middle. Av. *fri-n-3mna-2 pri-v-and*
Forms to be observed.

§ 590. The weak forms in *na*-(i. e. a-conjugation by transfer) are frequent; the instances of 3 pl. thus formed are noted above. Other examples of this transfer *(-n-a)* are given in the next section § 591.

§ 591. The transfers to the a-conjugation with weak stem *(no)* are: 1. Indicative. i. ACT. a. Pres. *hu-n-a-hi* 'thou pressest', *frin-a- 'ti, fri-n-S-mahi, fri-n-niti* (above).— ii. MID. *kir '-h-inte* 'they make, cut'.—b. Pret. i. ACT. *kir '-n-im* 'I made, cut', *sa-n-a-(* 'it appeared' (i. e. *sad-n-a(* § 185) Yt. 14.7.— ii. MID. *stir '-n-a-ta* 'he strewed'.

2. Imperative. i. ACT. GAV. *pir '-n-S* 'fulfil thou' Yt. 28.10, VAV. *mip-n-a-tu* 'let him turn', *fri-n-ititu* (above).—ii. MID.

*brt-n-avuha* 'cut thou'. 4. Optative. i. ACT. *kir'-n-oi-(, zara-n-al-ma* (GAV.) 'we might anger' Ys. 28.9, *stir'-n-ay-sn* 'let them strew'.—ii. MID. *stir'-n-al-ta* 'let him strew'. II. PERFECT-SYSTEM. Perfect.

(Cf. Whitney, *Skt. Gram.* § 780 seq.)

§ 592. General Remark. The chief characteristic of the perfect is the reduplication; the endings also differ in some respects from those of the present-system; the perfect shows likewise a distinction of strong and weak forms. As to signification, the perfect (and pluperfect) as 1 Vd. 5.59. — 2 *-Jmna* like 3-conj.

Personal Endings and their connection with the Stem.

§ 597-The endings of the perfect, especially in the middle voice, are mostly primary. They are attached directly to the tense-stem as in the unthematic conjugation; sporadic traces of a 'union-vowel' *i, 3* (cf. Whitney, *Skt. Gram.* § 797 seq.) perhaps however exist. See Bartholomae, *A.F.* ii. p. 97.

§ 598. The endings agree with those of the Skt.; some forms however are to be specially observed, see below § 599 seq.

Perfect Endings.

Perfect Endings (Observations). § 599. Singular:— First Person: ii. MIDDLE. A 1st. sg. mid. form in *-d* (i. e. *-au* § 54 = Skt. *-Su)* from a root ending in long *a* is perhaps to be found in *dado* 'I have made' Ys. 10.9 = Skt. *dadhau,* Whitney, *Skt. Gram.* § 800 e.

Second Person: i. ACTIVE. Note the form *-ta* (for *-pa* § 78 end) after *s* in GAV. *voistS* 'thou knowest'. § 600. Dual:—

Third Person: ii. MIDDLE. Observe the suffix *-te* 3 du. mid. in GAV. *dazdl* 'they both created' Ys. 30.4 (i. e. *dhazdhai, dha-dh-tai),* cf. Bartholomae, *h.Z.* xxix. p. 285 = *Flexionslehre* p. 16.

§ 601. Plural:—

Third Person: i. ACTIVE. The ending *-ir'S* (above) beside *-ar'* is found in GAV. *ci-kait-ir'l* 'they have thought, taught' Ys. 32.11.

Pluperfect (Preterite).

(Cf. Whitney, *Skt. Gram.* § 817 seq.)

§ 602. The existence of a preterite (pluperfect) indicative corresponding to the present perfect, seems to be shown by a few forms. There is, however, some uncertainty, see Note. The forms here recognized as pluperfect are made by adding the secondary endings directly to the perfect stem. The strong stem appears in the singular active; the weak stem elsewhere. The thematic *a* (transferring to the -inflection) is sometimes found.—Cf. Whitney, *Skt. Gram.* § 817 seq.

Note. There is much difficulty in distinguishing a pluperfect from some other reduplic. forms. Some of the examples may equally well be referred to other forms (impf., aor.) of the redupl. preterite.

Mode-Formation of the Perfect.

§ 603. The perfect like the other tense-systems shows an indicative (pres. perf.; pret. pluperf.), imperative, subjunctive (prim, and sec), optative and participle (cf. Whitney, *Skt. Gram.* § 808 seq.). These are formed as in the non-a-conjugation (unthematic); the subjunctive has the strong stem + mode-sign *a;* the optative has the weak stem + *-yd-,-1-.*

§ 604. A number of transfers to the -inflection instead of the thematic are found in pluperfect, imperat, subjunct, optative, and participle. See § 619.

Paradigm of the Perfect-System.

(Cf. Whitney, *Skt. Gram.* § 800 seq.)

§ 605. Examples of the inflection of the perfect may be taken from the following roots:—

Av. *fgarw-*'to seize' = Skt. *Ygrabk-;* Av. *fdviS-*'hate' = Skt. *ydvif-;* Av. *fi rud-*'grow' = Skt. *f 1 rudh-;* Av. *Ydars-* 'see'

Periphrastic Perfect. § 623. In YAV. traces of a periphrasis which may be construed as forming a perfect are found.— Cf. also Whitney, *Skt. Gram.* §§ 1070, 1072. In Av. the acc. sg. fem, of the pres. participle is united with the perfect of the auxiliary *ah-*to be:— YAV. *sral$ye'titim wvha(* 'it may have clung' (subjunct.), *astaraye'titim atvhSt* 'should have corrupted'.—Perhaps also here *biwivtSvha*

'he had frightened' Yt. i9.48,50 *()* nom. sg. ptcpl. *fbi 1 aw/ta,* cf. variants). III. AORIST-SYSTEM.

Aorist.

(Chiefly found in Gatha Avesta.)

§ 624. General Remark. In regard to form the aorist in Av. may perhaps best be denned as a preterite, whose exact corresponding present is missing and which consequently attaches itself to an analogous present and preterite, and forms a new system subordinate to these.

In regard to meaning the aorist in Avesta commonly denotes a simple past action, usually but not always momentary. It may often, as in Skt., be rendered by our 'have'.

The instances of aorist formation are found chiefly in the Gatha portions of the literature, but occurences in the later parts are by no means uncommon.

Note. The resemblance in form which the aorist bears to the preterite (imperfect) sometimes gives rise to question whether certain given forms are to be classed as preterite (imperfect) or as aorist; the decision depends chiefly upon whether or not we assume a present to the form— e. g. cf. Bartholomae, *Verbum* p. 63 seq.

§ 625. Two groups of aorists may conveniently be distinguished; they are i. non-sigmatic, 2. sigmatic. These comprise several sub-varieties of formation (7 as in Skt.), as follows.—Cf. Whitney, *Skt. Gram.* § 824.

1. Root-aorist.
i. Non-Sigmatic 2. Simple a-aorist (thematic).
3. Reduplicated aorist. ii. Sigma tic Aorist-System , 4. h-(s-) aorist.
5. ha-(sa-) aorist (or A-thematic). 6. //-aorist. 7. /-aorist.

§ 626. Augment and Endings. The augment in aorist forms as elsewhere in Av. is commonly missing; the augmentless forms, moreover, often have a subjunctive (imperative) signification (cf. § 445 Note 2 injunctive). The endings in the indicative are the secondary.

§627. Modes of the Aorist. The modes—imperative, subjunctive (prim., sec), optative:—of the aorist are formed according to the regular laws of the other systems.

Note. Observe the existence of a form 3 sg. i m p e r a t. mid. in *-qm* = Skt.

-*Sm:* GAV. *ir'iucqm* 'speak', *vidqm* 'it shall decide' Ys. 32.6, cf. Skt. *duhSm,* Whitney, *Skt. Gram.* § 618.

i. Non-Sigmatic Group.

§ 628. The aorists of the non-sigmatic group—1. rootaorist, 2. simple a-aorist (thematic), 3. reduplicated aorist —resemble preterites (imperfects) which correspond respectively to the root-class, the a-conjugation (thematic), and to the reduplicated class.

1. Root-Aorist. (Cf. Whitney, *Skt. Gram.* § 829.)

§ 629. The root-aorist is like an imperfect of the root-class without a corresponding present indicative. The endings are attached directly to the root in its strong or its weak form. The distribution of strong and weak stemforms is in general the same as in the present and perfect systems. The modes show their characteristic mode-signs.

§ 630. Example of root-aorist inflection (almost exclusively GAV.).

2. Simple o-Aorist (thematic). (Cf. Whitney, *Skt. Gram.* § 846 seq.)

§ 648. The instances of the simple a-aorist are not very numerous; in Av. this aorist plays a part similar to that in the Skt. of the Rig Veda. In formation and inflection it is identical with a preterite (imperfect) of the 6th class. The root in its weak form simply assumes the thematic vowel *a;* the secondary endings are then added for the indicative.—Cf. Whitney, *Skt. Gram.* § 846.

§649. Examples of the a-aorist (chiefly GAV.) are the following: 1. Indicative. i. ACT. Aor. (pret.) Sg. 3. *vida(* 'he found' (beside 3 sg. pret. *vitid-af),* *buja(* 'he absolved' (beside pres. *butij-a'titi).* — . MID. PI. 3. *jpH* 'they ruled' *(YiiS-).* 2. Imperative. i. ACT. Sg. 2. *vulS* 'find thou'. —ii. MID. PI. 3. *fyftntqm* 'let them rule'.

3. Subjunctive. i. ACT. Sg. 1. *hanani,* 3. /»OMt/'let me, him earn'. 4. Optative. ii. MID. Sg. 3. *fcalta* 'might he rule'. 5. Participle. i. ACT. *vtdafr* (in compounds). Likewise some other forms might be added.

Aorist Passive, third Singular. (Cf. Whitney, *Skt. Gram.* § 842.)

§ 667. In Av. as in Skt. an aor. 3rd. singular in *-i* with passive meaning oc-

curs, though it is not of common use. The form is made by adding *i* to the verbal root which has either the vrddhi or guna strengthening. The form may take the augment as in Skt.

§ 668. Examples of 3rd. sg. Aor. Pass. are the following:— (a) With vrddhi. — From Av. *fvac-* 'speak, call' *vSei,* *avaci* (GAV.) = Skt. *vdci, avdci;* Av. *fsru-* 'hear, call' *srSvi* (GAV.) = Skt. *srdvi;* so A v. *S'di* 'is said, spoken of /a/-(so Geldner) = Skt.

V. SECONDARY CONJUGATIONS. § 675. The secondary conjugations consist of the following formations (thematic), a. Passive, b. Causative, c. Denominative, d. Inchoative, e. Desiderative, and f. Intensive (unthematic).

A. Passive.
(Cf. Whitney, *Skt. Gram.* § 768 seq.) § 676. General Remark. The passive force may be given in any tense-system simply by employing the middle voice in a passive sense. In the present-system, however, there is also a formative passive made by means of the passive sign *-ya-*(cf. CI. 4) attached to the prepared root.

Note. The connection between this formative passive in *ya* and CI. 4 of the present-system is generally acknowledged. In Skt. the difference of accent distinguishes the two, the passive having accented *yd,* but CI. 4 an unaccented *ya.* As no written accent is found in Av., such a distinction cannot always be sharply drawn; it is therefore sometimes doubtful whether a given form is really a passive or merely a middle used with passive sense, e.g. *manyete* (pass.) Ys. 44.12 identical in form with *manyete* (mid.) Yt. 10.139 = Skt. *manydte, mdnyate.*

§ 677. Formation of the Passive. The passive sign is *-ya-*(= Skt. accented *yd-*) attached to the root which then assumes the weak form.

Note. The ar-roots require some remark as they frequently show MS. variations as to the way in which the radical r-vowel is expressed: e. g. Av. *ifmar-* 'to die', *mir-ye-'ti, mir-ye-'te, nur'-ye-'ti, ma'r-ye-'te* Vd. 3.33 = Skt. *mriydte;* again Av. *fkar-*'to make', *kir-ye-'ti* Yt.

10.109, *kir-ye-tite* v. I. *ka'r-ye-'tite* Vd. 3.9, cf. § 48 above. The development in such cases evidently is

Av. *mar-ya-te* (or *-a'r-*§ 48) Skt. *mr-'-yd-te* or *mir-ya-te (-'r-*§ 70) *mr-i-yd-tl*

§ 678. Endings. In Skt. the passive form assumes the middlei endings, but some exceptions with active endings occur, cf. Whitney, *Skt. Gram.* § 774. In Av. also, the middle endings are used but the active ones likewise are not very uncommon. Observe especially the MS. variants in final *e, i* (§ 35 Note 2) *kiryeHi, kirye'te.* The intransitive passive force seems therefore to lie in the *ya*element.

Note. An undoubted example of act. ending but passive force is *frS-yez-yS(* in Yt. 13.50 *kahe vd urva* (nom. masc.) *frayezya(* 'of which one of you will the soul be worshipped?' Apparently also with active ending (from *dayal* (subjunct.) Vd. 3.32, *ni-dayat* (impf.) Yt. 12. 17.

Modes of the Passive. § 679. The modes of the passive are the usual ones of the present-system; a complete list of forms, however, cannot be gathered from the texts.

Passive Inflection. § 680. Examples of passive voice with middle and active endings are the following: 1. Indicative. a. Pres. Sg. 3. *ba'r-ye'te* v. 1. *ba'rye'ti* 'he is borne', *kirye'ti* v. 1. *kirye'te* 'it is made'; PI. 3. *kirye'tite* v. 1. *ka'rye'Ute* 'they are made' (§ 48).— Pret. Sg. 2. *ma'ryavha* 'didst die' v. 1. *mir'yavha,* 3. *vt-sruyata* 'was heard', *ni-daya(* 'was placed'.

3. Subjunctive. Sg. 3. *ma'rya'te v.* 1. *mirya'te, mirya'ti* 'is destroyed, dies'; *yezya'te* 'is worshipped'; PI. 3. *ba'ryatite* 'they will be borne', *Janyatite* 'they will be slain' Yt. 14.43. 5. Participle. Av. *suyamna-*'being advanced, saved'. Note. From *fvar-*'to cover' is found a form *ni-vd'r-ye-'te* (v. 1. —on *B,* cf. § 39.

§ 681. A Perf. Pass. Participle in *-ta* or *-na* also belongs to the passive conjugation. See § 710 below,

§ 682. A Fut. Pass. Participle (Gerundive) in *ya-*is formed according to § 716 below.

§ 683. The Aorist Passive 3rd. Singular likewise falls under this formation. It is treated above, § 668.

B. Causative. § 684. General Remark. In Av. as in Skt. the causative *C-aya-)*, like the Denominative is identical in form with CI. 10, the latter being originally a causative formation. The causal is found in the Present-System.

Note. In Skt. many of the so-called causatives do not have a strict causative value and are therefore reckoned as belonging to the Skt. *cur*Class(io); similarly in Av., a number of causative forms have been treated above under Class 10, cf. § 482 seq.

§ 685. Formation. The present-stem of the causative is formed by adding the causal formative element *-aya*to the root which is usually strengthened. The strengthening of the root is subject to certain variations.

a. Internal or initial *a* before a single consonant is generally lengthened (vrddhi), but sometimes it remains unchanged, thus: Lengthened *S*, Av. *fvat-*'to comprehend', caus. 'make known' *vStaya-*= Skt. *vataya-;* Av. *ftap-*'to warm, be warm', caus. 'make warm' *tS-paya-*= Skt. *tSpdya-;* Av. *fgam-, jam-*'go, come' *jSmaya*— Skt. *gSmdya-* (Whitney, *Skt. Gram.* § 1042 g).—Unchanged *S*, Av. *fpat-*'to fall, fly' *pataya-* = Skt. *patdya-;* Av. *fsad-*'appear' *sa-daya-*= Skt. *chaddya-;* Av. *fap-*'obtain', *Upaya-*, opp. to Skt. *apdya-*. b. Internal and initial *a* before two consonants (i. e. long by position) remains unchanged: Av. *ydafyS-*'to know, cause to know' *daft$aya-*= Skt. *daksdya-;* Av. *fvaS-*'grow, cause to grow' *valaya-*= Skt. *vaksdya-;* Av. *Yb"-*'bind' *batidaya-*= Skt. *bandhdya-;* Av. */zamb-*'crush' *zim-baya-*= Skt. *jambhdya-*. c. Final long *a* disappears: Av. *ystS-*'to stand, cause to stand' *staya-*opp. to Skt. *sthapdya-,* cf. Whitney, *Skt. Gram.* § 1042 i. d. Internal or initial *i, u* before single consonants (i. e. in light syllables) have the guna-strengthening: A v. *yvid-*'to know', caus. 'inform' *valdaya-*= Skt. *vlddya-;* Av. *fruc-*'light up' *raocaya*—— Skt. *rocdya-*. e. Final *u* (or *i*) receives the vrddhi-strengthening: Av. *fsru*'to hear' *srSvaya-*= Skt. *srSvdya-*. Note 1. The nasal of the present-stem (CI. 9)

appears in Av. *hr'ntaya-*from *ykart-*'to cut' as in Skt. *krntdya-,* cf. Whitney, *Skt. Gram.* § 1042 h. So also Av. *buti-jaya-*from *fbuj-*'to release'. Note 2. The root *za-*'to let go' makes *za-yaya-,* cf. Whitney, *Skt. Gram.* § 1042.

Note 3. Observe with lengthening instead of strengthening of root (§ 61 Note) GAV. *"rapaye'titt* 'they cause pain' *(Yrup-)* = Skt. *ropdyanti;* GAV. *"raddyatS* 'he caused to lament' = Skt. *rodhdyata.*

Modes of the Causative. § 686. The Causative shows the same modes, 1. Indicative, 2. Imperative, 3. Subjunctive, 4. Optative, including also 5. Participle, as the present-system naturally does.

Inflection of the Causative: Present-System. § 687. The causal in the present-system is inflected after the a-conjugation (thematic), see CI. 10 above, §§ 481, 482 seq.

Other Causative Formations.

§ 688. To the causal formation belongs not only the causative of the present-system, but also a causal aorist (see § 652); possibly likewise a causative perfect (pluperfect), and some other parts.

§ 689. On the reduplicated Causative Aorist, see § 652 above.

§ 690. Possibly here belongs as Periphrastic Perfect (Plupf.), Av. *bi-wivavha* 'he had frightened', see § 623.

§ 691. A causal derivative from *fhap-*'to sleep' is made by attaching the root *da-*'to make, do' in its causal form directly to the radical element; thus, Av. *habdaye'ti* 'puts to sleep'.

§ 692. Other causative derivatives made with root *da-*(cf. § 691) but without causal form, are *ava-vhab-dalta* 'he would cause to sleep' *fhap- ty-aoidat* 'caused to howl' *(yfirus-), yaoida'ti* 'makes pure' *fyaoi-).*

§ 693. Some forms with causal signification but without the *-aya*formation occur: Av. *va$a(* 'he caused to grow' Ys. 48.6 opp. to *valaya-to* 'they both cause to grow' Ys. 10.3.

§ 694. An occasional verbal noun (infinitive) or adjective (participle) is likewise to be noted under the causal formation: Av. *frasruta-*'made

E. Desiderative.
(Cf. Whitney, *Skt. Gram.* § 1026 seq.)

§ 699. The desiderative in Av. resembles the Skt. in formation and signification. The root is reduplicated and the formative element *-ha (-vha, -/o, -za)* = Skt. *-sa* as desiderative sign is added. The vowel of the reduplicated syllable is always *-i-(-i-*§ 21 Note); the initial consonant of the root in reduplicating follows the usual rules above § 465.

The root of the desiderative appears ordinarily in its weak grade; sometimes, however, in its strong (middle)

F. Intensive.
(Cf. Whitney, *Skt. Gram.* § 1000 seq.)

§ 702. The characteristic features of the Intensive are reduplication and the unthematic inflection. In formation, the Intensive in Av., as in Skt., closely resembles the reduplicating class (CI. 3) of the present-system; it is distinguished from CI. 3 by having a strengthened reduplicated syllable.

§ 703. As regards the reduplication, the formation of the Intensive in Av. is twofold.

VI. VERBAL ABSTRACT FORMS.
Participle, Gerund, Infinitive.

§ 708. To the verbal system there also belong the Participle or verbal adjective, the Gerund, with Gerundive, and the Infinitive or verbal noun.

A. Participle.
1. Participle in *-atit,-at* (Act.); *-mna,-ana* (Mid.).
(Cf. Whitney, *Skt. Gram.* §§ 583, 584 etc.)

§ 709. Participial forms in *-atit,-at* (i. e. *-nt),* fem, *-a'fiti,-a'tt* in the Active, and forms in *-mna,-ana (-ana)* in the Middle, are found in each tense-system. As these attach themselves directly rather to the tense-systems, they have been discussed above under the respective systems, cf. §§ 488, 533 etc.

2. Passive Participle in *-ta.*
(Cf. Whitney, *Skt. Gram.* § 952 seq.)

§ 710. A passive participle or past passive participle, is made in Av., as in Skt., by adding the suffix *-ta* = Skt. *-td* (accented) directly to the verbal root, which is subject however to certain euphonic changes. This verbal adjective in *-ta* (m. n.), *-td* (f) is regularly declined according to the a-declension §§ 236, 243. Examples of the formation are Av. *pata-*'protected' (*//o-*) = Skt. *pdtd-; Av. gar'pta-*'grasped' *tygarw-§ 74) = Skt. *grbhHd; Av. drufyta-*'deceived' *(tfdruj-§ 90)* = Skt. *drugdhd-*.

§ 711. Treatment of the Root before *-ta.* The form of the root is subject to modification and is liable to vary before the added suffix. The following points may be noted:— 1. The root very commonly (but not always) shows the weak form, if it has one, before *-ta;* a penultimate nasal is accordingly dropped. Thus, with weak form, from Av. *fvac-* 'to speak' ptcpl. *"ufyta-*= Skt. *ukta-;* Av. *yhn-*'press out' *huta-*= Skt. *sutd-;* —Av. *fpatij-*'draw, drive' *pata-;* A v. *fhfaifj-*'encircle' *hafyta-*= 5. Perfect Middle Participle in *-Sua,-Sua.*
(Cf. Whitney, *Skt. Gram.* § 806.)

§ 715. On the formation of the Perf. Mid. Participle, see above under Perfect-System, §§ 611, 618.

B. Gerundive and Gerund.

1. Gerundive: (a) Fut. Pass. Participle in *-ya* (declined). (Cf. Whitney, *Skt. Gram.* § 961.)

§716. A declined derivative adjective with verbal force is made from some verbs by attaching the formative element *-ya* to the root. Such an adjective is regularly inflected according to the a-declension. In meaning, it often corresponds to the Latin form in *-ndus;* it is therefore commonly called a gerundive or future passive participle.

Examples are from Av. 'to wish', a gerundive (vbl. adj.) *ijya-*— Skt. *ifya-;* A v. *fkars-*'draw furrows, plow' *hr$ya-* = Skt. *"krfya-;* A v. *fvar-*'choose, believe' *va'rya-*= Skt. *vdrya-.* Other instances occur.

2. Gerundive: (b) Fut. Pass. Participle in *-tva,-pwa* (declined). (Cf. Whitney, *Skt. Gram.* § 966 a.)

§717. A declined derivative adjective of like signification *(-ndus)* with the preceding (§ 716) is made by adding *-tva,-piva,-dwa* (§§ 94, 96; see also under Suffixes) directly to the root in its strong form. Such a verbal adjective is regularly inflected after the -declension.

Examples are: A v. *jqpiva-*'worthy to be killed' (*j/ya«-*) = Skt. *hantva-;* Av.

*fy$naopwa-*'worthy to be satisfied' (A£/«««-*); Av. *varltva-*'to be done' (J/-z/arz-), *mqpwa-*'to be thought', *vaffdwa*'to be spoken'.

3. Gerund (Absolutive) in *-ya* (indeclinable). (Cf. Whitney, *Skt. Gram.* § 989 seq.) § 718. A species of Gerund or Absolute (indeclinable) in *-ya* seems to occur in the following instances with *da'pe:* A v. *a'biga'rya* 'seizing' = Skt. *"girya;* Av. *pa'tiricya* 'throwing away'. But cf. Bartholomae in *B.B.* xv. 237. VII. PERIPHRASTIC VERBAL PHRASES.

§ 722. In the Av., there is an inclination occasionally to use periphrastic phrases made up by means of an adj., a participle or a noun, with a copula verb or auxiliary, instead of a regularly formed tense-stem. The auxiliary may sometimes even be omitted. The periphrastic phrase is chiefly found in YAV.; its presence, however, is recognized in GAV.— Cf. Whitney, *Skt. Gram.* § 1069 seq.

§ 723. The possible existence of a Periphrastic Perfect has been noted above, § 623.

§ 724. A number of Periphrastic Expressions made by means of an adjective, a participle, or a noun combined with a verb, deserve special mention.
1. Periphrastic with Av. 'to go' = Skt. cf. Whitney, *Skt. Gram.* § 1075 a. GAV. *stavas ayeni* 'I shall praise' Ys. 50.9. 2. With Av. *yah-*'sit' = Skt. *YSs-,* and Av. *ysta-*'stand' = Skt. *YsthS-,* cf. Whitney, *Skt. Gram.* § 1075 c. YAV. *upa.ma'ttm Sste* 'remains', *te hiStetiti jiar'jzarnitil* 'they keep flowing'. INDECLINABLES.

§ 725. General Remark. The indeclinable words in Avesta, correspond in general to those in Sanskrit and in the other Indo-Germanic languages. Under Indeclinables are comprised Adverbs, Prepositions, Conjunctions, and Interjections. These may be taken up in detail.

A. Adverbs.

§ 726. The adverbs in Av., as in Skt., may be made either from a pronominal stem or from a noun-stem by means of a suffix, or their forms are merely crystallized cases of old or abandoned nouns.
1. Adverbs made by Suffix. (Cf. Whitney, *Skt. Gram.* § 1097.)

§ 727. A number of adverbs are made

by adding suffixes to a noun or an adjective stem, or especially to a pronominal stem. Their meaning is various.
a. Adverbs of Place. (Cf. Whitney, *Skt. Gram.* §§ 1099, 1100.)

§ 728. The principal adverbs of place made by means of a suffix are:

S uffix Av. *-to* — Skt. *-tas,* Av. *a'witd* 'around' = Skt. *abhitas.* —Suffix *-pra* — Skt. *-tra,* A v. *kupra* 'where' = Skt. *kutra;* Av. *hapra* 'along, with'= Skt. *satrd.*—Suffix *-da* = Skt. *-ha,* Av. *ida* 'here, now' = Skt. *iha.* Likewise a number of others.
b. Adverbs of Time.
(Cf. Whitney, *Skt. Gram.* § 1103.)

§ 729. The number of temporal adverbs that are made by means of a suffix is not extensive but corresponds in proportion to the Sanskrit. Examples are:

B. Prepositions.
(Cf. Whitney, *Skt. Gram.* §1123 seq.)

§ 734. Prepositions in the sense of words that 'govern' oblique cases do not strictly exist in Avesta, any more than in Sanskrit. There are, however, a number of adverbial words which are used with the oblique cases and which define such cases more precisely. Their office is thus directive. These are termed Prepositions, and sometimes they seem really to govern the cases with which they stand.

§ 737. The abl. phrase YAV. *atitara( nalma* 'within' is employed, in addition to its adverbial use, also with a force that is practically equivalent to a preposition: Av. *atitara( nalmS( ySr'drijd* 'within a year's time'; *atftara( naema( baripri$va* 'within the wombs'.

C. Conjunctions.
(Cf. Whitney, *Skt. Gram.* § 1231 seq.)

§ 738. The conjunctions and particles of adverbial value have in part been treated above under Adverbs. It remains only to emphasize the conjunctive force of some of the most important Co-ordinates and Subordinates. They are mostly postpositive in position.
1. Co-ordinate Conjunctions.

§ 739-The chief co-ordinate conjunctions, copulative, adversative, etc. are here noted.
a. Copulative. A v. *ca* 'and, que' = Skt. *ca;* A v. *ca... ca* 'both... and' = Skt. *ca..*

. *ca;* Av. *uta* 'also' = Skt. *uta;* Av. *uta... uta* 'both... and' = Skt. *uta... uta.* Negative, Av. *noi(* 'not' = Skt. *nid;* Av. *noi(.. . noi(, noi(... nalda, nava... noi(* 'neither. .. nor'. b. Adversative. The only one in use seems to be A v. *Id* 'but, however' = Skt. *tu.* c. Disjunctive. Av. *tS* 'or, else', e.g. Vd. 12.1 = Skt. *vS;* Av. *vS... vS* 'either... or' = Skt. *vS... vS.* d. Causal. Av. *zi* 'for' (orig. asseverative, and often so used in Av. as in Skt.) = Skt. *hi.* e. Illative. Here may be noticed Av. *apa* 'so, therefore' = Skt. *dtha.* Perhaps also some others. 2. Subordinate Conjunctions.

§ 740. The subordinate conjunctions, temporal, modal, final, etc., with adverbial force, have been noted above under Adverbs (§ 728 seq.), e. g. Av. *yada* 'when', *yapa* 'as, that', etc. To these may be added the conditional conjunction Av. *yezi, yedi* 'if = Skt. *yddi.*

D. Interjections.

§ 741. A few exclamations are worthy of notice; they are, in part, remnants of cases of unused words crystallized as Interjections. Examples are not numerous.

§ 742. The most important Interjections are: Av. *at* 'O' (w. voc.) = Skt. *at;* Av. *usta* 'hail' (an old loc.). Likewise a few others, probably originally caseforms of nouns or adjectives, e. g. Av. *dvoya* 'alas' (old instr.), cf. *dvoya me bdvoya* 'woe, woe indeed to me' Yt. 3. 14; Av. *inja* 'ha, here', *tinja* 'ho, there'. WORD-FOR MAT I ON. FORMATION OF DECLINABLE STEMS.

§ 743. General Remark. Words are made from roots either directly without an affix, or they are more commonly formed by means of added suffixes, or again by composition.

(1) Only a small proportion of declinable stems, however, are made directly from verbal or pronominal radicals in their bare root-form without any affix. The simple root does sometimes serve as a declinable stem (see discussion below, § 744), but this happens chiefly in compounds. (2) The great majority of words, in Av. as in other tongues, is derived from radicals by assuming an affix (suffix or prefix). The root-part of the word contains the fundamental idea;

the prefix or suffix modifies its meaning. (3) A third method of making new words is by combining words already formed so as to build up a compound.

The formation of verbs and pronouns has been sufficiently treated above; attention is here given to the formation of noun-words.

i. Suffixless Formation.

Root-Words.

(Cf. Whitney, *Skt. Gram.* § 1147.) § 744. A limited number of declinable stems, nouns and adjectives, in Av. as in Skt, are made directly from a simple root without assuming any suffix. The suffixless stems have been discussed above, under Declension §§ 248, 261 etc. They occur oftenest as finals of compounds; they are therefore frequently made up with verbal prefixes.

As to signification, the root-words, as in Skt. (cf. Whitney, *Skt. Gram.* § 1147 a), are action-words, especially infinitives; or they may be nouns of agency. Sometimes they are adjectives.

§ 745. As examples of Root-Words without Suffix may be given:

Av. *vac-*'voice, word' = Skt. *vac-;* Av. *druj-*'deceit, Fiend' = Skt. *druh-;* Av. *adruh-*'undeceiving' = Skt. *adruh-;* Av. *a'wi-ac-*'following' — Skt. *abhi-fdc-.*

Note 1. In Av., as in Skt., root-words at the end of a compound are subject to some variation, (a) Internal i is often lengthened, *anufhac-*'attending'. — (b) Radical *i, u* remain unchanged. — (c) Roots ending in a short vowel including *-ar* usually assume a *t,* as in Skt. (cf. Whitney, *Skt. Gram.* § 1147d), A v. *afor't*-title of a priest *fbar-),* cf. Skt. *bhft-,* Whitney, *Skt. Gram.* § 383 h. Similarly in the prior member of a compound, Av. *srut.gao$a-*'of listening ears' (j/jr«-), cf. Skt. *srut-karpa-;* Av. *ji-fa$a-*(V»-), cf. Whitney, *Skt. Gram.* §§ 1147e, 383 b.

Note 2. Reduplication is perhaps to be sought in Av. *ta-tuc-,* cf. loc. pl. *tu-tuh$va* Vd. 6.51, cf. Skt. *tvdc-.* 2. Derivation by Prefix and Suffix. (Cf. Whitney, *Skt. Gram.* §§ 1118, 1136.) § 746. Words are derived from radicals chiefly by the addition of prefixes and suffixes. The Prefixes and

Suffixes may now be taken up in detail. PREFIXES. a. Nominal Prefixes, Substantive and Adjective. (Cf. Whitney, *Skt. Gram.* § 1121.)

§ 747. A number of prefixes are used in making new words of substantival or adjectival value out of words already formed; these may be called nominal or noun *fra* 'forth, fore, forward', *ybar--- frS* 'bring forth' = Skt. *pr& pa'ti* 'towards, against, back', *fbar--(-pa'ti* 'bring towards' = Sk. *prdti vi* 'apart, away, out', *fbar---vi* 'bear asunder' = Skt. *vi kqm, hati-,* GAV. *him, hiti-*'together', *Ybar---hqm* 'bear together' = Skt. *sdm.*

Note. Instances of stereotyped caseforms of a noun entering into verbal combination as prefix, are to be found: e. g. Av. *yaoS -(-fda-, yaoi-da'ti* 'makes pure', cf. Av. *yaoS* Ys. 44.9 = Skt. *yos.*

§ 751. The connection between the prefix and the verb, in Av. as in Vedic Skt. (Whitney, *Skt. Gram.* § 1081) is very loose; several words, therefore, often intervene between the prefix and the predicate, so that sometimes it is difficult to tell whether the prefix is to be connected directly with the verb or is to be regarded merely as an adverb: e. g. *apa haca qzahibyo i mipra barois* 'mayest thou, O Mithra, bring us away from distresses' Yt. 10.23, beside *apabara'ti* 'he brings away' Vd. 5.38.

§ 752. A repetition of the prefix is not uncommon, that is, the prefix may stand at some distance before the predicate and then be repeated in combination with the verb:

As an example of such repetition compare, Av. *hqm ida $aet3m hqm. baray3n* 'let them collect possessions together there' Vd. 4.44.

Note 1. In GAV., the metre shows that the second prefix is regularly to be expunged: e.g. GAV. *hya( him voha ii mazda him'-fraS/S manavha* 'when he conferred with Vohu Manah' Ys. 47.3. Again *hya( Pwa hfm ca$ma'ni hnij-grabim* 'when I conceived thee in mine eye' Ys. 31.8., Similarly *us... uz-Jln* Ys. 46.12; et al.

Note 2. In the case of a long predicate, when several subjects or objects belong to the same verb, the verb itself is sometimes expressed but once, the prefix being then repeated each time with the subject or object as the case may be: e. g. *aya dalnaya fraoritita i ahurd mazdcb a$ava fra vohu ma no, fra... fra... ftS...* 'Ahura Mazda professed his faith according to this law, Vohu Manah professed it, so did' etc. Ys. 57.24.

§ 753-When the prefix immediately precedes the verb to which it belongs, the form of the prefix is sometimes SUF-FIXES.

§ 755. Most derivatives, in Av. as in other languages, are made by means of suffixes. These resemble the corresponding suffixes/in Skt., and they may likewise be divided into two general classes: a. Primary Suffixes, or those added directly to original roots or to words resembling such.
b. Secondary Suffixes, or those added to derivative stems which have already been formed with a suffix.

These two classes may now be taken up in detail.

A. Primary Derivatives.

(Cf. Whitney, *Skt. Gram.* § 1143.)

§ 756. A Primary Derivative is a word that is formed by adding one of the so-called Primary Suffixes directly to an original root.

§ 757. Form of the Root. The root to which the primary suffix is added may undergo more or less change in its form. Most generally the root is strengthened either to the *guiia* or the *vrddhi* stage. Such variations for the most part answer to corresponding changes in Skt.; they will n o t be taken up in detail here; reference may be made to Justi, *Handbuch der Zendsprache* pp. 366—383.

§758. Some general remarks, subject to exceptions, however, may be made with regard to the strengthening of the root.
(a) In Av., as in Skt., internal radical *a* is commonly vrddhied before the suffix *a;* but it commonly remains unchanged before the suffix /. (b) Internal and initial *i, u* are gunated before the suffix *a* and *i.* (c) Internal and final /, « are gunated before the sufftxes *-ana,-ah,-pra,-pwa,-man.* (d) The root generally remains unstrengthened before the suffixes *-ta,-ti,-*

*u,-pu,-ra,-van,* and in some other cases. The Principal Primary Suffixes.
(Cf. Whitney, *Skt. Gram.* § 1146 a.)
§ 759. A list of the principal primary suffixes may here be given in connection with the Sanskrit, see Whitney, *Skt. Cram.* § 1146 a. One or two of these here given might perhaps be further resolved and regarded as secondary, but it is found convenient to include them here.

A few other Primary Suffixes.

§ 760. A few other suffixes occur sporadically and may also for convenience be classed under the primary division, though their secondary origin may be possibly traced. As examples may be taken:

Suffix, Av. *-aya* in *zar'daya-;* Av. *-Sra* in *daara-;* Av. *-ura* in *razura-;* Av. *-tah* in *parStSh-*(Whitney, § 1152 a). Likewise some others.

Discussion of the Primary Suffixes.
1. Av. *-a* = Skt. *-a* (Whitney, § 1148). § 761. With this suffix a great number of derivatives are formed. Their signifl-cation is various; they are adjectives, action-nouns, agent-nouns. The root is generally strengthened by *guna* or *vrddhi.* Examples are very numerous:

Noun (masc, neut.). Av. *vdza-*'strength'= Skt. *vdja-;* Av. *maeja-*'cloud'= Skt. *tneghd-;* Av. *gaofa*'ear' = Skt. *ghd$a-;* Av. *cafyra-*'wheel' (neut. ) = Skt. *cakrd-.*—A d j e c t i v e. Av. *ama-*'strong' = Skt. *dma-;* Av. *asdra-*'headless'; Av. *am3$a-*'immortal' = Skt. *amfta-;* Av. *draoja-*'deceitful' = Skt. *drogha-.* Also many others.
2. Av. *-an* = Skt. *-an* (Whitney, § 1160). § 762. This suffix forms a limited number of neuter and masculine nouns of action and agency, including also a few adjectives. Examples are:
Noun. Av. «£/a«-m. 'ox'= Skt. *ukfdu-;* Av. *ta/an-*m. 'shaper' = Skt. *tdksan-;* Av. *"rvan-*m. 'soul'; Av. *masan-*n. 'greatness' = Skt. *mahan-.* — Adjective. Av. *ivitidan-*'not receiving'; Av. *ta"rvan-*'conquering'.
3. Av. *-ana (-3nd)* = Skt. *-ana* (Whitney, § 1150).
§ 763. This suffix, as in Skt., forms many derivatives, nouns and adjectives of varied value. Roots in *i, u* commonly

receive the #«rt-strengthening before this suffix. Some of the adjectival derivatives made with this element can hardly be distinguished from participles. Examples are:

Noun. Av. *vavkana-*n. 'clothing'= Skt. *vdsana-;* A v. *hanjamana-*n. 'assembly' = Skt. *sqgdmana-;* Av. *bajina-*n. 'dish' = Skt. *bhSjana-,* § 17, 30; A v. *malpana-*n. 'dwelling'; Av. *raocana-*n. 'light, window' = Skt. *rocana-.*— Adj. Av. *zayana-*'wintry'. § 764. After an *r,* the Av. form *-ina* answers in some instances to orig. *-ana,* while in others it corresponds to *-na* (i. e. *- 'na,* see § 802). These must be distinguished. As examples after *r:* (a) Av. *-ina* = Skt. *-ana* (i. e. *-ana),* Av. *varma-*m. 'choice, belief = Skt. *varand-;* Av. *hamirina-*n. 'battle, conflict' = Skt. *samdrana-.* Likewise some others. But observe Av. *karana-(-ana)* 'side, shore' Yt. 5.38 etc. opp. to Av. *kar'na-(-na)* 'ear' Yt. 11.2 = Skt. *kdrna-;* yet consult the variants. (b) Examples of Av. *-ina* (i. e. *- 'na)* = Skt. *-na,* after *r,* are given below under *-na* § 802. 4. Av. *-a'ni* = Skt. *-ani* (Whitney, § 1159). § 765. Sporadic traces of the suffix *-ani* in Av., as in Skt., are to be found. As example may be quoted: Av. dui-*a'ni*-adj. 'evil' Vd. 14.5.
5. Av. *-atit (-atit,-ifit)* = Skt *-ant* (Whitney, § 1172). § 766. This is the suffix which forms the pres. and fut. participles. It has been sufficiently treated above, §§ *477, 514* 6. Av. *-ar (-ara)* — Skt. *-ar* (Whitney, §§ 169 a, 1151 1). § 767. This suffix forms a limited number of nouns; they are almost all of the neuter gender. It occurs likewise in adverbs and prepositions, probably there representing old case-endings. In some nouns the form becomes *-ara* by the a-transfer. The prefix *-ar* must be connected with *-an,* cf. § 337. Examples: Av. *vadar-*n. 'weapon' = Skt. *vddhar-;* Av. *zafar-*n. 'jaw'; Av. *balvar-, baivara-*(-inflection) 'thousand'; Av. *nar-, nara-*m. 'man' = Skt. *ndr-, nara-.* Observe the adverbs Av. *antar'* 'between, inter' = Skt. *antdr;* Av. *i$ar'* 'immediately'.
7. Av. *-ah* = Skt. *-as* (Whitney, § 1151). § 768. From this very common suffix, in Av. as in Skt., a great number of

derivatives are made. They are chiefly abstract neuter nouns and some adjectives (probably originally distinguished from the latter by a difference of accent, cf. Whitney, *Skt. Gram.* § 1151 e). The roots in *i, u* show /za-strengthening before this suffix. Examples are: Noun. Av. *avah*-n. 'aid' = Skt. *dvas-;* Av. *aenah*n. 'sin' = Skt. *enas-;* Av. *t3mah*-n. 'darkness' = Skt. *tdmas-;* Av. *raocah*-n. 'light'. — Noun, Adjective. GAV. *dvae$ah*-n. 'hate', *dvae$ah*-adj. 'hateful' Ys. 43.8 = Skt. *dve$as-;* Av. *vasah*-n. 'will', *vasah*-adj. 'willing' Ys. 31.11, cf. Whitney, *Skt. Gram.* § 1151c A feminine noun in Av., as in Skt., is Av. *u$ah*-f. 'dawn' = Skt. *usds-,* cf. § 357 above. 8. Av. *-a* = Skt. *-a* (Whitney, § 1149). § 769. This suffix makes feminine adjectives answering to masculine and neuter a-stems. It also makes a considerable number of feminine actionnouns. Its form is often obscured, as it frequently appears as *a* §§ 25, 17,18. Examples have been given under declension of fem. nouns and adjectives §§ 362, 243. 9. Av. *-ana (-ana)* = Skt. *-ana* (Whitney, § 1175). § 77-This suffix is used in forming middle and passive participles; it has therefore been treated under the different tense-systems, §§ 477, 507 etc. Examples of participles mid. and pass, are:
Av. *isdna*-'ruling' = Skt. *isdna-;* Av. *mauhdna*'thinking' (aorist ptcpl.); Av. *yazdna*-'worshipping', *pap3r'tana*-'fighting'. Also others.

Note. A few noun-stems in *-an* also show *-Stm* as a sporadic heavy form with a-transfer, e. g. *ar$ana*-'male' § 310.
10. Av. *-i* = Skt. *-i* (Whitney, § 1155). § 771. With this suffix a considerable number of derivatives are formed. They are adjectives and substantives. The masculines are chiefly agent-nouns; the feminines are abstracts; there is an occasional neuter. The root generally shows the *guna* stage. Examples are:
Nouns. Av. *azi*-m. 'dragon' = Skt. *dhi-;* Av. *kavi*-m. 'Kavi, king' = Skt. *kavi-.*—Av. *karfi*-f. 'circle, circuit' = Skt. *kr$i-;* Av. *dahi*-f. 'creation' = Skt. *dhasi-;* Av. *tnaeni*-f. 'wrath, punish-

ment' Ys. 31.15, 44.19 = Skt. *mem-.*— Av. *a$i*-n. 'eye' = Skt. *dk$i-.* —Adjective. Av. *za'ri*-'yellow, golden' = Skt. *hdri-;* Av. *darfi*-'bold', etc.
§ 772. On Av. *-ita* = Skt. *-ita,* see § 786 below.
§ 773. On Av. *-iti* = Skt. *-iti,* see § 789 below.
11. Av. *-in* = Skt. *-in* (Whitney, § 1183). § 774. Only a few undoubted instances of this suffix as a primary derivative are noted; its use in secondary formation of possessives is more familiar (§ 835), though not so common as in Sanskrit. Quotable examples of the primary usage of this suffix are:
Noun. Av. *kainin*-f. 'maiden'.—Adjective. Av. *"tacin* (in *afltacino)* 'flowing, running'.
12. Av. *-ina* = Skt. *-ina* (Whitney, § 1177 c).
§ 775-There are a few quotable derivatives that show this suffix. Examples are:
Adjective. A v. *Jafma*-'right' = Skt. *ddkfina-;* Av. *za'rina*'golden' = Skt. *harina-.* 13. Av. = Skt. *-is* (Whitney, § 1153). § 776. A small number of neuter nouns are made by means of this suffix. Instances are:
Noun. Av. *bar'zil*-n. 'cover, mat', cf. Skt: *barhis-;* Av. *hadM*-n. 'abode'; Av. *vipil*-n. 'judgment', *sna'pil*-n. 'weapon', cf. § 359 above.
14. Av. *-igi* = Skt. *-ifi* (cf. Whitney, §§ 1153, 1156 a).
§ 777-This suffix belongs perhaps rather under secondary derivation than under primary endings. It occurs in only one or two words and may best be mentioned here. It seems to answer as a corresponding feminine formation 21. Av. *-tar C-dar)* = Skt. *-tar* (Whitney, § 1182). § 787. This suffix is used in forming masculine, and a few feminine, nouns of agency and relationship, cf. §321 seq. The suffix is attached directly to the root; and radical *i, u* are generally strengthened before it. There is a corresponding feminine *-prl* besides. Examples of *-tar* are: (1) Nouns of Agency. Av. *ddtar*-m. 'giver, creator' = Skt. *d(h)dtar-;* Av. *zaotar*-m. name of priest = Skt. *hotar*-et al. — (2) N o u n s of Relationship. Av. *patar*-m. 'father' — Skt.

*pitdr-;* Av.*mdtar*f. 'mother' = Skt. *mdt-dr-.*
Note 1. The suffix *-tar* is sometimes disguised (cf. § 163): Av. *kS$ar*-m. 'eater'; Av. *bS$ar*-m. 'rider' = Skt. *bhartar-.*
Note 2. Observe the form of the suffix in YAV. *dujdar-,* GAV. *dug'dar*-f. 'daughter' Yt. 17.2, Ys. 45.4 = Skt. *duhitdr-.*
Note 3. Observe *-tar* as neuter in infin. YAV. *vtdoipre* Yt. 10.82 (perhaps here *har'pre* v. 1. Ys. 62.2).
22. Av. *-ti* = Skt. (Whitney, § 1157).
§ 788. This suffix is used in forming a large number of feminine nouns, chiefly abstracts, and also an occasional masculine noun or adjective. The suffix is added directly to the root in its weak form. Examples are numerous: Noun. Av. *anuma'ti*-f. 'thought, agreement' = Skt. *dnumati-;* Av. *cisti*-f. 'wisdom' = Skt. *citti-;* Av. *stit'ti*-f. 'praise' = Skt. *stuti-;* Av. *supti*-f. 'shoulder' = Skt. *sup-ti-;* Av. *paHi*-ma sc. 'lord' = Skt. *pdti-.*— Disguised form, Av. *afi*-f. 'Rectitude' = *ar-ti* § 163. § 789. A form Av. *-iti* = Skt. *-Hi* (Whitney, § 115 7 g) is found in a few words: Av. *spa$iti*-Yt. 19.6, *askl'ti*-(cf. § 32) Ys. 44.17.
23. Av. *-tu* = Skt. *-tu* (Whitney, § 1161). § 790. With this suffix, in Av. as in Skt. , are formed a number of abstract and concrete derivatives. They are prevailingly masculine. The root is commonly strengthened before the *-tu.* Examples are: 33. Av. *-ma* = Skt. *-ma* (Whitney, § 1166). § 808. With this suffix a considerable number of derivatives are made; they are adjectives and nouns. The nouns are chiefly masculine. The root is often strengthened. Examples are:
Noun. Av. *haoma*-m. 'haoma'-Skt. *soma-;* Av. *al$ma*-m. 'fury'; Av. *"rup-ma*-m. 'growth'. — Av. *gar'ma*-n. 'heat' = Skt. *gharma-.*— Adjective. Av. *bSma* 'shining' = Skt. *bhama-;* Av. *tama*-'strong, swift'; Av. *gar'ma*-'hot' = Skt. *gharma-.* 34. Av. *-man* = Skt. *-man* (Whitney, § 1168). § 809. The suffix *-man* in Av., as in Skt., forms a number of derivative action-nouns; most of these are neuter; a few are masculine. The root generally shows the gunas-trengthening. Examples are:

Noun. Av. *asman*-m. 'stone, heaven' = Skt. *diman*-; Av. *rasman*-m. 'column, rank'.—Av. *nSman*-, *nqman*-n. 'name' = Skt. *ndman*-; Av. *valsman*-'dwelling' (in *valsmm-da* Yt. 10.86) — Skt. *vis-man*-; Av. *taofyman*-n. 'seed' = Skt. *tokman*-; A v. *bar'smau*-n. 'barsom'.

35. Av. *-mi* = Skt. *-mi* (Whitney, § 1167). § 810. This suffix, as in Skt., is found in a very few masculine and feminine nouns. Examples are:

Av. *var'mi*-m. 'wave, billow' = Skt. *armi*-; Av. *dqmi*-m. 'creator' Ys. 31.8; Av. *"zami*-m. 'birth' = Skt. *Jam/*. — Av. *bumi*-f. 'earth' = Skt. *bhumi*-, *bhumt*-.

36. Av. *-mna,-mana* = Skt. *-mana* (Whitney, § 1174)§ 811. This suffix is used in forming the middle (passive) participles of the different systems. It has been discussed above, § 709 etc. Furthermore on Av. *-mna,-mana* (Gk.-;y.evo;) opp. to Skt. *-mana,* see § 18 Note 2.

37. Av. *-ya* = Skt. *-ya* (Whitney, § 1213). § 812. This suffix is used in making the Gerundive (fut. pass, ptcpl. § 716) and also verbal adjectives; likewise a few nouns. It is sometimes difficult, in Av. as in Skt., to distinguish the primary from the secondary deri 46. *Av.-vah(-vtSvh-,-us)* = *Skt.-vas(-vqs,-us),* Whitney,§ 1173.

§ 822. With the suffix *-vah (-vtxvh* str. , *-us* wk.) is made the perfect active participle. The root is reduplicated except in a few words which make the perfect without reduplication. For examples, see § 348 seq.

47. Av. *-var (-vara)* = Skt. *-vara* (Whitney, § 1171). § 823. With the suffix *-van (-vara)* are made a considerable number of neuter nouns. They commonly show a parallel stem with suffix *-van* (§ 820). The form *-vara* arises by transfer to the a-declension. Examples are:

Av. *kar$var*-n. f. beside *kar$van*-'clime, zone'; Av. *zafar*-(i. e. *zap-var* § 95) n. beside *zafan*-'jaw'; Av. *bdevar*-n. beside *baevan*'myriad'. So *mipwara*-n. *(-vara)* beside *mipwan*-'pair'. Observe Av. *srvara*-(for *sruvara*-§ 68) 'horned, Sruvara'.

B. Secondary Derivatives.
(Cf. Whitney, *Skt. Gram.* § 1202 seq.)
§ 824. The so-called Secondary Suffix-es are those which are added to make new derivatives from primary derivatives or words which already show a suffix. The forms thus arising are termed Secondary Derivatives. The great majority of them are adjectives, but often they are nouns.

§ 825. Form of the Stem. In assuming the secondary suffix the stem, though it is already prepared, may still undergo other changes in form.
(a) Final-a of a stem disappears before suffixes beginning with a vowel or *y*.
(b) Final-;, *-u* of a stem are generally strengthened before suffixes beginning with a vowel, though *u,* as in Skt., sometimes remains unchanged, cf. Whitney, *Skt. Gram.* § 1203 a, b. (c) Final *-an* of the stem appears as *-an,-n,* depending chiefly upon the difficulty of pronunciation (cf. Whitney, § 1203 c): Av. *bar'smanya*-'relating to the barsom', *vySfa'riya*-'ruling in the council'; Av. *vSr'prajni*-'victorious' (from a«-stem), cf. Skt. *vartraghna*-. (d) The initial syllable of the stem receives the v r d d h istrengthening in secondary derivation less often in Av. than in Skt., cf. Whitney, § 1204. Examples of vrddhi (cf. § 60) are: Av. *Shu'ri*-'of the Ahurian', cf. Skt. *dsuri*-; A v. *mazdayasni*-'belonging to the worship of Mazda'; Av. *gSvya*-beside *gaoya*-'belonging to the cow', opp. Skt. *gdvya*-(§ 60 Note d); Av. *hSvani*'relating to Havana'; Av. *SrSlya*-'belonging to a spear'. For gunaforms, see above § 60 Note c.
The Principal Secondary Suffixes.
(Cf. Whitney, *Skt. Gram.* § 1207.)

§ 826. A list of the principal secondary suffixes may here be given in connection with the Sanskrit, see Whitney, *Skt. Gram.* § 1207.

A few other Secondary Suffixes. § 827. A few other secondary suffixes occur sporadically and may for convenience be mentioned here.

Suffix. Av. *-$va* in numerals, *pri$va*-'a third', *capru$va*-'a fourth', *pavtavhva*-'a fifth' Ys. 19.7. Also Av. *-sa* = Skt. *-sa* (Whitney, § 1229), Av. *navasa*-, *i$asa*-, *al$asa*-. 1. Av. *-a* = Skt. *-a* (Whitney, § 1208).

§ 828. This sufnx, in Av. as in Skt., is very common. It forms secondary derivatives from nouns or from adjectives. The derivatives thus made are chiefly adjectives denoting 'relating to', 'of', 'with'; but there are also numerous nouns, including patronymics.

The secondary *a* is especially common in compound words, transferring the whole compound to the tf-declen *za-wrot3ma*-. The treatment of the stem-final before these endings has already been given. Examples, see §§ 364, 374.

15. Av. *-tat* = Skt. *-tat* (Whitney, §§ 1238, 383k). § 842. This suffix makes feminine abstracts. Its independent origin is shown, for example, in *Av.yavaeca.td'te* beside *yavaetaHaeca* Ys. 62.6, Yt. 13.50, cf. § 893. Examples:

Av. *uparatSt*-f. 'supremacy' = Skt. *up-ardtSt*-; A v. *ha"rvatat*-f. 'completeness, Salvation' = Skt. *sarvdtat*-. Likewise others.

16. Av. *-ti* = Skt. *-ti* (Whitney, § 1157I1). § 843. The suffix *-ti* appears as secondary ending in a few words; the most important of these are the numerals. Examples are:

Av. *panwar'ti*-f. 'bow' (cf. *panvar*-); Av. *fi$valti*-'sixty' = Skt. *fafti*-; Av. *hapta'ti*-'seventy' = Skt. *saptati*-; Av. *nava'ti*-'ninety' = Skt. *navati*-, see § 366 above.

17. Av. *-pa (-da)* = Skt. *-tha* (Whitney, § 1242 d). § 844. The secondary suffix -*pa* is to be sought in one or two numeral and pronominal words. As examples: Av. *haptapa*-'seventh' = Skt. *saptdtha*-; Kv.*putyia*-'fifth', cf. Skt. *pattc-a-tha*-;—Av.*avapa*-'thus, so'. 18. Av. *-pya* = Skt. *-tya* (Whitney, § 1245 b).

§ 845. This suffix in Av., as in Skt., makes one or two derivative adjectives from prepositions and adverbs. As instances: Av. *a'wipya*'away, distant'; Av. *pascq'pya*-'behind'.

19. Av. *-pwa* = Skt. *-tva* (Whitney, § 1239).

§ 846. With this sufftx, as in Skt., a few neuter nouns denoting 'condition', 'state' are formed from adjectives and nouns. Examples:

Av. *avhupwa*-n. 'lordship'; Av. *ratupwa*-n. 'mastership'; Av. *vavhup-wa*-n. 'good deed' = Skt. *vasutvd*-. 20. Av. *-pwana* = Skt. *-tvana* (Whitney, § 1240).

§ 847. This suffix is hardly more than an extension of the preceding, which it resembles in meaning. A quotable example is the abstract noun, Av. *na'ripwana*-n. 'marriage', cf. Skt. *patitvand-,* Whitney, § 1240.

21. Av. *-na* = Skt. *-na* (Whitney, § 1223 g). § 848. With this suffix a very few secondary derivatives are formed. Examples are: FORMATION OF COMPOUND STEMS.

§ 858. General Remark. Compounds, Verbal and Nominal, occur in Avesta as in Sanskrit, but in Av. since most words are written separately in the MSS. and each is followed by a point, the compounds are not always so easily recognized as in Skt., nor are the rules of Sandhi so rigorously carried out.

Verbal Composition has been sufficiently treated above, § 749 seq.; it is necessary here to take up only the NounCompounds.

Note. In printed texts the compounds are differently marked in different editions; Geldner's Avesta has the compound united in printing and retains the separating point (.); Westergaard likewise but a small dash (-) is used; Spiegel's edition does not designate the compounds.

NOUN-COMPOSITION.

§ 859. Noun-compounds have either a substantival or an adjectival force. They consist usually of two members, more rarely of three (§ 894), e. g. *drva-a$a-cipra* 'the sound offspring of righteousness'. The members which enter into composition may be nouns, adjectives, or indeclinables; or they may be parts of a verb, either radical or participial. The final member of the compound receives the inflection. The first member is subject to some modification in form, generally assuming the weak grade.

§ 860. Examples of different combinations, nouns, adjectives, etc., entering into composition are: noun-compound is much looser than in Skt.; hence the frequent variations in the form of the prior member. Observe particularly that the first member often assumes the form identical with its nominative singular. The principal points may be presented in detail.

§ 865. Final -*a* of the stem may remain unchanged before consonants, but more often it appears as -*d* like the nominative. Occasionally, though more rarely, it is lengthened. Examples are:

Av. *hazavra.gao$a-, hazavro.gao$a-, hazavra.gao$a-*'thousandeared' Yt. 17. 16, Yt. 10.91, Yt. 10.141 etc. So *hti-, hva-*'self in composition, *hSdSta-*'self-governed', *hvSvastra-*'self-clothed'. Note. Observe that *a* when preceded by *y* may give *ya, yd, ya,* but sporadic traces of reduction (§ 67) are found, e. g. Av. *na're.manah(na'rya--m")* 'manly-minded' Ys. 9.11, beside *ha'pyS.data-*Yt. 11.3, *ha'pya.var'z-.* Similarly traces of « for *va, va* are found in Av. *var'dusma*'soft-earth' *(var'dva-).*

§ 866. Original *S* of feminine stems may remain unchanged, but sometimes, like *a*, it becomes -*o*. Examples are:

Av. *daina.vazah*-nomen propr., *daend.disa*-m. 'teacher of the law' *(dalna-), urvaro.bal$aza*-adj. 'having the balm of plants' *(urvara-).*

Note. Original *ma* (prohibitive) appears as *mS*-in composition in YAV. *makasvtl mastri* 'no dwarf, no woman' et al. Yt. 5.92; GAV. *mavalpa-*'not failing' Ys. 41.1.

§ 867. Final *i, t, u, (u)* of a stem remain as a rule unchanged in the prior member of a compound, though *t* usually appears for *i.* Examples are:

Av. *za'ri.gaona*-'yellow-colored' *(za'ri-), multi.masah*-'large as the fist' *(muSti-), na'ri.cinah*-'seeking a wife' *(na'ri-).* — Av. *asu.ka'rya*-'quickly working', *vo"ru.gaoyao'ti*-'having wide pastures'. Note 1. The «-stems occasionally show-«/, like the nominative singular: e. g. Av. *bazul.aojah*-'strong-armed' (observe-/), *nasul.ava. bsr'ta*'corpse-defiled'. Somewhat different is the-/ in Av. *anuS.hac*-'accompanying' (Skt. *anusdc),* Av. *pasul. ha"rva*-'cattle-protecting', see above § 754, 2. Observe also YAV. *nasuspacya*-'corpse-burning' (with j-before § 754).

Note 2. Av. *gau-, gao*-'cow' appears in composition as *gao-, gava-, gavo*-(cf. Whitney, *Skt. Gram.* § 361 f): e. g. Av. *gaoyao'ti*-'cow-pasture' = Skt. *gdvyuti-; * Av. *gavahti*-'abode of cows', A v. *gavo.stana*-'cow-stall' = Skt. *gosthana-.*

§ 868. Simple stems ending in *p* show forms identical with the nominative singular. Examples are:

Av. *aftcipra-*'containing the seed of waters' *(ap-), awidata*'contained in the waters', *kir'fShvar-*'corpse-eating' *(kihrp-).* § 869. The a#/-stems as a rule show the weak form -*a(* as final of a prior member. Sometimes, however, they show -*o,-as,* like nominative, § 295. Examples are:

Av. *ralva(-aspa-*'having splendid horses', *var'da(.galpa-*'increasing the world'.—Av. *bard.zaopra-*(observe-o), beside *bara(.zaopra*(observe -*af)* 'bearing the libation' Yt. 10.30, Yt. 10.126; *raevas.cipra-*'of splendid family' (but cf. also § 151). Note. Observe the form *th* instead of / in Av. *zarathultra-*'Zoroaster', *hamaspapmaldaya*-name of a season.

§ 870. The a«-stems show *a* in composition as in Sanskrit (cf. Whitney, *Skt. Gram.* § 1315a), or they appear as -*o.* Examples are:

Av. *a$avajan-*'slaying the righteous' *(a$avan-), nqma.azba'ti*'invocation by name', *rama.$ayana-*'having an abode of repose' *(raman-).*—Beside Av. *ramo-liti-*'abode of repose' *(raman-), zrvo.dSta-*'created in eternity' *(zrvan-).* § 871. The ar-stems naturally have anaptyctic (') § 72, and form respectively *ar', 3r'.* As examples may be noted:

Av. *ayar'.bara-*'day's journey', *hvar'.bar'zah*-'height of the sun'; — *nir'.bar'zah*-'height of a man'. Observe commonly *atir'.pata-, Stir'.savah-, Stir'*-etc. Yt. 13.102, but *atravaa*-name of priest Vsp. 3.6 etc. § 872. The a-stems may appear in their original form -*as* under certain circumstances (§ 110), but otherwise they become -*d* as usual (§ 120). Examples are:

Av. *timascipra-*'containing the seed of darkness', *manaspao'rya*'having the mind pre-eminent'.—Av. *ayd.fyaoda-*'having a helmet of iron' *(ayah-), savo. gaipa-*'useful to the world', *har'no. dah-*'glory-giving'. Note 1. Observe *z* (§ 170) in Av. *vavhazdSh-*'giving what is better' Ys. 65.12. Remark also the weak form of -*vah* in *Av.yaltuI.gao*-nomen propr. Yt. 13.123, *viduS.yasna*-'knowing the Yasna'.

Note 2. Observe the peculiarity *(-ah* retained) in *mipahvaca* 'falsespeaking' *(mipah--4-v)* Ys. 31.12.

c. Treatment of the final Member. § 873. The final member of a compound in Av. as in Skt. (cf. Whitney, *Ski. Gram.* § 1315) often undergoes changes in its original inflection; these will be noticed in the following in detail.

§ 874. There is a special tendency for the final member of a compound to assume the o-inflection; a compound is often thus transferred from the consonant to the vowel declension (cf Whitney, *Ski. Gram.* § 1316c). Examples are: Av. *hvar'.dar's̄a-*(Skt. *svardfs-)* 'sunlike', beside *pard.dar's̄-, paro.dar's̄a-;* Av. *atir'.vaia-*title of a priest, beside *Stir'.vaS̄*(cons.).

§ 875. An o«-stem in the final member often undergoes transformation, as in Skt. (cf. Whitney, *Skt. Gram.* § 1315). As examples may be taken: Av. *capru.capna-*(observe *-a)* 'four-eyed', beside *baevar'.ca$mana*(observe *-and)* 'thousand-eyed', from *cabman-.* § 876. The final member sometimes undergoes abbreviation, owing to an original change of accent in assuming the weak form, or to other causes (cf. Whitney, *Skt. Gram.* § 1315). As examples: Av. *upasma-*'upon earth' *(z'm-),* *frabda-*'fore part of the foot' *(pada-),* *fraf$u-*'abundance of cattle' *(pasu-).* Likewise others.

d. Case-form appears in prior Member.

§ 877. In Av., as in Skt. (cf. Whitney, *Skt. Gram.* § 1250), a case-form is sometimes found in the prior member of a compound. Examples are: a. Accusative (especially before radical finals). Av. *aham.mir'nc-*'destroying the soul', *ahmaoja-*'confounding righteousness' *(ahm maoja, m -(-m = m, § 186),* *ahumbiS̄-*'healing the soul', *daeum.jan-* 'daeva-smiting'. — b. Dative. Av. *yaval-ji-*'living for ever'. — c. Genitive. Av. *z'mascipra-*'having the seed of earth'. — d. Locative. Av. *duraldars-* 'seeing at a distance', *rapalSta-, rapailtar-*'warrior standing in a chariot' *(rapt-), ma'dyoi.pa'tiltana*'to the middle of the breast'.

Classes of Compounds.

(Cf. Whitney, 5/. *Gram.* § 1246 seq.) §

878. Modelled after the Sanskrit Grammar the compounds in Avesta may conveniently be divided into the following classes:— i. Copulative. SYNOPSIS ( H. Determinative J?ePundcnt Descriptive.

*it* iv. Other Compound Forms. Final. These different classes may be taken up in detail in comparison with the corresponding Sanskrit divisions. i. Copulative Compounds. (Cf. Whitney, *Skt. Gram.* §§ 1252, 1255.) § 879. Copulative Compounds (Skt. Dvandva). Two co-ordinate terms which would form a pair connected by 'both — and' may dispense with the conjunction and unite into a compound. The Av. Dvandva-Compounds differ from the Skt. in this that in Av. each member assumes the dual form and is separately declined. Examples of Copulative or Dvandva-Compounds are: Av. *pasu vtra* 'cattle and men' Ys. 9. 4 etc.; *pasubya virae'bya* 'by cattle and men' Vd. 6.32 etc.; *pasvat viraya* 'of both cattle and men' Vsp. 7.3 etc.; *apa urva're, ape urva're* 'water and trees' Ys. 9.4, Gah 4.5; *payii pwdr'ltara* 'the keeper and the judge' Ys. 57.2. Note. A rather late instance may be cited in which several successive members, though ordinarily found only in the singular, unite as a series each in the plural and form an aggregate compound: Vsp. 10.1 *ayese yesti ar3zahibyu savahibyj fradafubyo vidadaf$ubyd vo'lru.bar3stibyd vo"ru.jar'stibyo aheca kar$vanJ ya( hanirapahe.* ii. Determinative Compounds.

(Cf. Whitney, *Skt. Gram.* § 1262 seq.) § 880. Determinative Compounds are divided into two classes, (a) Dependent Compounds, (b) Descriptive Compounds. In regard to signification, the Determinative may have either a substantival or an adjectival value.

a. Dependent Compounds. (Cf. Whitney, *Skt. Gram.* § 1264 seq.) § 881. Dependent Compounds (Skt. Tatpurusa) are those in which the former member stands in relation to the latter member as though it were governed by the latter. The force of the prior member is that of an oblique case (ace, instr. gen. etc.) depending upon

the latter; and actual case-forms in such instances do sometimes occur, see § 877 above. The compound has noun or adjectival value according to its final member.

1. Noun value (Whitney, § 1264): Accusative relation. Av. *miprd.druj-*m. 'one that breaks his pledge'. — Gen. relation. Av. *vispa'ti-*m. 'lord of the clan'. — Loc. relation. Av. *rapalUa-*m. 'warrior standing in a chariot' *(rape* = actual loc., cf. § 877). 2. Adjective value (Whitney, § 1265): Acc. relation. Av. *kamir'dd.jau-*'smiting the head'.—Dat. relation. *hs.damida.ta-*'created for all creatures'.—Instr. relation. Av. *ahuraddta-*'made by Ahura'. — Abl. relation. Av. *qzo.tuj-*'freeing from distress'. — Loc. relation. Av. *z'ntar'guz-*'hiding in the earth'. b. Descriptive Compounds. (Cf. Whitncy, *Skt. Cram.* § 1279 seq.)

§ 882. Descriptive Compounds (Skt. Karmadharya) are those in which the former member stands not in a case-relation but in attributive relation to the second and adds some qualification to it. The value of the compound itself is substantival or adjectival according to its final member.

1. Noun value (Whitney, § 1280 b, d): Av. *dar'jo.fti-*f. 'a long residence', *pir'no.mtSvha-*n. 'full-moon';—Av. *ustradaenu-*f. 'she-camel', cf. Whitney, *Skt. Gram.* § 1280 d. 2. Adjective value (Whitney, § 1282): Av. *vispo.lamya-* 'allbrilliant', *upard.ka'rya-*'making higher, raising up'. With advbl. preftxes (o-, an-, hu-, duS-, arl-etc.), Av. *hukir'ta-*'well-made', Av. *arlufyda-* 'right-spoken'. Likewise some others. Hi. Secondary Adjective Compounds. (Cf. Whitney, *Skt. Gram.* § 1292 seq.) § 883. The secondary adjective compounds are of two kinds, (a) Possessive, (b) those with governed final member. a. Possessive Compounds. (Cf. Whitney, *Skt. Gram.* § 1293 seq.)

§ 884. Possessive Compounds (Skt. Bahuvrlhi) are composite adjectives formed from a corresponding Determinative compound (§ 880) merely by adding to the latter the idea of 'having' or 'possessing' that which the determinative itself denotes.

§ 885. The Skt. shows a difference

of accent between a Determinative and its corresponding Possessive; in Av., as there is no written accent, the distinction cannot be drawn in that manner.

§ 886. The second member of the Possessive is generally a substantive; the first member may be a substantive, adjective, pronoun, numeral, participle or indeclinable. The force of the compound always remains adjectival.

Possessive Adjectives. — Noun initial. Av. *aficipra-*'having the seed of waters'. — Adj. initial. Av. *dar'gd. Lazu-*'having long arms, longimanus'. —Pron. initial. Av. *hviivastra-*'having own clothing', *ya.$yaopna-*'having what actions' Ys. 31.16. — Num. initial. Av. *hazavra.gao$a-*'having a thousand ears' (cf. Whitney, § 1300). — Ptcpl. initial. Av. *uzgsr'pto.draf$a-* 'with uplifted banners'.— Indecl. initial (Whitney, § 1304). Av. *ahafna-*'not-sleeping', *ahvyama'*having excessive might' (Whitney, § 1305).

b. Adjective Compounds with governed final Member. (Cf. Whitney, *Skt. Gram.* § 1309 seq.)

§ 887. These adjectives are exactly the reverse of Dependent compounds; they are attributives in which the first member practically governs the second member. The second member is always a noun and stands in case-relation to the first. The compound itself has an adjectival value.

This group shows two subdivisions, (1) Participial, (2) Prepositional, according as the prior member is a participle or a preposition. Details follow.

1. Participial Adjective Compounds. (Cf. Whitney, *Skt. Gram.* § 1309.) § 888. These compounds are old in Av. as they are in Sanskrit. The prior member is a present participle which in meaning governs the second part. The whole is an adjective. Examples are:
Av. *vana(.paana*-adj. 'winning battles', *var'daf.gaepa-*'increasing the world', *vikir3(.ustana-*'cutting off life'. Likewise in nomina propria *haeca(.aspa-* 'Haecataspa'.

2. Prepositional Adjective Compounds. (Cf. Whitney, *Ski. Gram.* § 1310.) § 889. These are combinations in which the first member is a preposition (ad-

verb) that governs the second member in meaning. The whole is equivalent to an adjective. Examples are:
Av. *afy$nu-*'reaching to the knee', cf. Skt. *abhijnu-*(Whitney, § 1310a); Av. *a'wi.daliyu-*'around the country', *atftar'.daliyu-*'within the country' (cf. Skt. *antarhastd-),* Av. *uzdaliyu-*'out of the country'; Av. *upasma-*'upon the earth' *(z'm-*§ 152); Av. *pard.asna-*'beyond the present' (i. e. *pari)* -(-*azan-*) § 153, cf. Skt. *paroksa-;* Av. *taro.yara-*'beyond a year', cf. Skt. *tiroahnya-.* iv. Other Compound Forms.

§ 890. Beside the above regular compounds, in Av. as in Skt., there are also some other composite forms that require notice.
a. Numeral Compounds. (Cf. Whitney, *Skt. Gram.* § 1312.)
§ 891. Numeral Compounds (Skt. Dvigu) are a species of determinative that have a numeral as prior member, and which are commonly, though not always, used as a singular collective noun in the neuter gender. Examples are:
Av. *prigaya*-n. 'space of three steps', *pripada*-n. 'three feet, a yard', *nava. kar$a*-n. 'the nine furrows', *nava./igapara*-n. 'space of nine nights'. — Av. *patica.yafystts* (f e m. acc. pl.) 'five twigs'. — Av. *hapto'ritiga* (masc. plur. ) 'the Great Bear'.
b. Adverbial Compounds. (Cf. Whitney, *Skt. Gram.* § 1313.) § 892. Adverbial Compounds (Skt. A vyayibhava ) are composites made by the union of a preposition or a particle as prior member and a noun as final member, combined to form an indeclinable noun or rather neuter accusative used adverbially, cf. § 934. The class is quotable in an instance or two: Av. *aprittm* 'up to three times', cf. Skt. *advadaidm;* Av. *pa'tySpsm* 'against the stream, contrary' (§ 934) Ys. 65.6, Vd. 6.40 = Skt. *prattpam* (cf. Lanman, *Skt. Reader* p. 195); Av. *fra.apam, nySpsm, upa.Spim* 'from out, down, to the water' Vd. 21.2.
c. Loose Compound Combinations. (Cf. Whitney, *Skt. Gram.* § 1315.)
§ 893. One or two other points in regard to compounds and their formation may be noticed here.

1. The nomen propr. *na'ryo.savha*-m. 'Nairyosangha' sometimes has its component elements separately declined, e. g. *na'ryehe savhahe* Yt. 13.85, Vsp. 11. 16, beside *na'ryo.savhahc* Ny. 5.6. Similarly, the derivative *yavneca.ta'te* beside *yavaeta'talca* 'for ever' Ys. 62.6, Yt. 13.50, cf. § 842. So in verbal derivatives, *zarazd5-, zarasca da(,* etc. 2. Observe later such agglomerations, especially from initial words of chapters (cf. Te Deum), as A v. *kamnamalzqm ha'tim* 'the whither-to-turn Chapter' *(kant mmoi zqmj* Ys. 46 end; *ta(.pwa. psr 'sa'*beginning with the words This-I-ask-Thee'. Likewise in nomina propria, resembling the Puritanical names, e. g. Av. *a$im.yeuhe.raoca nqma* 'Bright-in-Righteousness by name' Yt. 13.120, et al.

§ 894. Long compounds are not common in Avesta; as examples merely may be quoted, Av. *frddat.vispqm.hujyd'ti-* 'advancing all good life', *na'ryqm.hqtn. var'tivatit'*having manly courage', *pouru.sar' do.vird.vqpwa* 'having a crowd of many kinds of male offspring' Vsp. 1.5.

Sandhi with Enclitics.
(Cf. Whitney, *Skt. Gram.* § 109 seq.)
§ 95-The principles of euphonic combination may be regarded as twofold: (1) as applied in the building up of a word from its elements; (2) in the union of words in a sentence. The former may be called Internal Combination or Word-Sandhi; the latter, though practically wanting in Av., is called External Combination or Sentence-Sandhi.

§ 896. The laws for the internal combination of formative elements and endings have been treated above under Phonology.

§ 897. Sentence-Sandhi, or the external combination of words in a sentence, is wanting in the Avesta (§ 4) except in the case of enclitics and in compounds, and there only conditionally. The words otherwise are written separately, each followed by a point. Thus, GAV. *yapd aim* Ys. 27.13; GAV. *ywsca uHl* Ys. 39. 3; YAV. *ni am3m* Ys. 9.17; YAV. *a'pi imam* Ys. 57.33, and countless others.

Note 1. In Geldner's *Metrik* pp. 54— 57, numerous instances are collected where external sandhi is apparently to be accepted, but they are uncertain, and in the edition of the Avesta texts Geldner has rightly followed the MSS.

Note 2. Observe the MS. reading GAV. *zi(* 'for indeed' (but in metre properly *zi i()* Ys. 45.8. Conversely GAV. *y.ipSiS* (so also according to metre, but better MS. authority for *yapa Sis,* Geldner) Ys. 33. 1.

Combination with Enclitics and Proclitics.

§ 898. Instances of Sandhi are common in the case of enclitics like *tit, he, cif, ca* which form a unit with the preceding word and are often written together with it; but even here the manuscripts often preserve the usual law of keeping each word separate and unchanged. As examples: YAV. *patriae* 'round him' (combined like Skt. *hi sa/t* Whitney, *Skt. Gram.* § 188) Ys. 9.28, beside *ni him* (uncombined) Yt. 13.100. Again YAV. *sfotidam fe mand k3r'nu'di* 'make his brain cracked' Ys. 9.28; GAV. *kas.te* 'who to thee' Ys. 29.7; GAV. *kas-nd* (cf. Germ, 'man') Ys. 44.4. So GAV. *sasfoti-cd* (observe *n)* Ys. 53.1 beside *uzufy$yqn-ca* (observe *n)* Yt. 13.78.— Similarly with Sandhi after the manner of enclitics and proclitics, GAV. *huzti-tuss sp3tito* Ys. 43.3; YAV. *havayms' tanvo* 'of his own self'; GAV. *vasas' fys-aprahyd* Ys. 43.8; YAV.*yas' tafymo* 'I who am strong' Yt. 19.87; YAV. *uHyao-jand* 'thus speaking', beside *u'ti aojand.*

Note 1. In the MSS., enclitics and proclitics are frequently written together as a single word, e. g. GAV. *kSmsni* for *kS. mi.nS* Ys. 50.1; *topwS* for *ta.pwS* Ys. 31.13; *tftigS* for *titfg.S* Ys. 46.13; *na'riva* for *na'ri.vS* Ys. 41.2. Likewise YAV. *Stag* and *a.ta(* Vd. 5.2, and many others.

Note 2. Observe that *-ca* 'que' is always written together with the preceding word; notice the difference of treatment of vowels and consonants before it. See *(Sea,-Sca,-ica,-asca,-asca,-Ssca)* §§ 19, 26 Note, 120, 124, 129.

§ 899. Special attention may be drawn to the treatment of words before an enclitic beginning with *t.* In several instances, especially in the Gathas, a word before a /-enclitic takes a sort of

compromise form made by a mixture of the usual pause form and the grammatical Sandhiform. Thus are to be explained: GAV. *vista* (compromise between *vas.ta* and *vi ta,* hence *s)* Ys. 46. 17; GAV. *yatigstu* (mixture of *yaug tu* and *yqs.tu).* Contrast GAV. *akSs-tStig f— Ss--tJ* Ys. 50.2, with A v. *gaipas-ca (as--c).* But GAV. *das-tu* Ys. 28.7, cf. § 124 above. Note. Observe likewise YAV. *kas'.pwqm, yas'jnvS,* a compromise between *ko pwqm* and *kastvqm* etc. § 78 above.

§ 900. The laws of euphonic combination in NounCompounds and also in Verbal-Composition have been treated above §§ 753, 861 seq.; they require no further remark here.

(The Sketch of the Syntax and Metre follows in Part Indexes to

Part I

I. AVESTA-INDEX (Grammatical Elements).

The references throughout are to the sections (§§).

Abbreviations are extensively used; but it is believed they will be readily recognized. For example, 'cpd.' is compound, 'cpsn.' composition; 'dcln.' means declension; 'endg.' ending; 'pronc.' pronunciation; 'primy.', 'scdry.' ' stand for primary, secondary; 'pdgm.' is paradigm; etc.

The Indexes are comparatively full, but if an element is not found under one of its letters look for it under one of its other letters, or under the appropriate head in the other Indexes. Remember that long and short vowels sometimes interchange in Avesta.

*a,* pronc. 6; = Skt. *a* 15; for Skt. *S* 17; interchanges with *S (i)* in MSS. 18 N., 472 N., 498; labialized to *o* 38, 39; strengthened or contracted 60; str. in causat. 685; lost after *n, r;* etc. in denom. 696 N.; loss of in scdry. deriv. 825 a; a-anaptyctic 72. a-stems, dcln. 236; transfer of -, «-stems to a-dcln. 256 N., 269. *a-,* pronom. stem 422 seq., 431. a-conjugation (themat.), in general 469-506; classification and formation 470; class (first) of verbs 470, 478-507; (sixth) 470, 479-507 i (fourth *ya)* 470, 480-507; (tenth *ayd)* 470, 481 till 507; transfer from root-class 529; transfer from

redupl. class 563-5, 573; transfer from ««-, III. GENERAL INDEX.

Ablative, the ending -*St* lightened to -*ll(* 1 g, 239; remarks on formation 222 seq. ; advl. use of 731.

Abbreviation of final member of compound 876.

Absolutive (gerund) 718.

Accents, not written in Av. MSS. 2; effect of 265, 341, 885.

Accusative, formation 222 seq.; neut. sg. in pronouns 379; as infinitive 721; as adv. 731; in compounds 877, 881.

Active endings with passive force 678 N.

a-declension, transfer from cons. dcln. 344; from *vah stem* 351; from a/»-stem 355, 357 N. 3; from //-stem 359 N. See also Transfer.

Adjective, dcln. of adj. 219 seq.; pronominal dcln. 443; comparat. degree 345-o. 3&3 se1-' adj-Prefixes 747-8; formed by primy. and scdry. derivation 761 seq.; adj. denoting material 829; adjective cpds. 881-3, 887-

Adverbial prefixes 733; advl. uses of prep. phrase 737; adverbial cpds. 892.

Adverb, numeral 375; multiplicative 376; pronominal 436; formation of adv. 726-32; shows case-forms 731-

Agency, nouns of 787.

Agglomerations 893.

Aggregative compounds 879 N.

Alphabet, characters and translitera-tion 1.

Anaptyxis 2 N., 69, *72.*

Anusvara (Skt.), how represented in Av. 46.

Aorist-system, synopsis and formation 447-8, 624-68; radical aor. subjunct. 549; augment missing in aor. 626; has scdry. endings 626; modes of aor. 627; redupl. aor. 650-2; causative forms 652; sigmatic aor. 653 seq.; passive aor. 3 sg. 667-8.

Aspiration, pronunciation of *h 12.*

Aspirate mediae-(-*t* or-J-*S* 89.

Assimilation of consonants 185.

Augment, rules for in Av. 466; common omission of aug. 466, 626; restored for metre 466 N. 2.

takes the place of strengthening 685 N. 3; lengthening before -vaiit 857 N. 1.

Ligature, written in MSS. 3; hm, h, hv 3. 13-

Liquid, pronc, of r 11; / wanting in Av. 11 N.; nature of r 100.

Locative, formation 222 seq.; loc. infinitive 721; as adverb 731; in compounds 877, 881.

Loss of a consonant 187-8.

Loose compound combination 893.

Material, formation of adj. denoting material 829.

Mediae (g, d, b,j), pronc. 8; character 82; med. aspirate --l or --s 89.

Members of compound 861-77.

Metathesis of r 191.

Metre, shows augment 466 N. 1; shows dropping of prefix 752 N. 1; shows Sandhi 753 N. 1, 897.

Middle voice 445 N. 1; with pass. force 676; mid. pass. ptcpl. 811.

Mode, in verbal inflection 445; formation 459 seq.; indic. 459; imperative 460; subjunct. 461-2; opt. 463-4; in a-conj. 473 seq.; in non-a-conj. 510 seq.; in perf. 603-4; 'n aorist 627; in future 670; in passive 679.

Monosyllables, long 24.

Nasals, pronc. 11; character 101; in 7th class of verbs 470, 554-65; in causative 685 N. 1.

Nasalization of a (a) to q 45, 46, 201.

Neuter, endings 225-7; acc. sg. of pronouns 379; form interchanges with fem. 232, 383.

Nomen proprium, formation 893.

Nominative, sg. fem. -e for orig. -ya 67; formation 222 seq.; in first member of cpd. 864, 867 N. 1.

Non-a-conjugation, formation 516-92.

Non-sigmatic aorist 628-52.

Noun-declension, 219 seq.; composition S59-95.

nu-(fifth) class of verbs 470, 566-74.

Number, remarks on 220.

Numerals 366-76; cardinals 366; formation 367-8, 374; num. adverbs 375; multiplicatives 376; in-/a 844; in -ma 849; numeral compounds 891.

Optative, mode-formation 463; endings 464; of a-conj. 476, 504-5; of non-a-conj. 514; of redupl. class 552.

Ordinals—see Numerals 366 seq.

Original (--sonant 47 seq.

Pada-endings, -biS,-bts 22, 85.

Palatal i — A v. s, /, I 145 seq.

Palatalization of s (a) to i 30, 491, 593 (0-

Participle, dcln. pf. act. 348; general formation 446, 477, 709-15, 822; of a-conj. 475, 506-7; pf. pass. ptcpl. 681, 710 seq.; fut. pass, ptcpl. 682; causal 694; forms in -atit,-mna,-ana 709,811; passive in -ta 710-11, 786; -ita 712; -na 713, 802; participial adj. compounds 888.

Passive voice 445 N. 1; aor. 3 sg. pass. 667-8; form, and pdgm. 676-9; endings 678; pass, force with act. endings 678 N.; modes of the pass. 679; fut. pass. ptcpl. 681-2; pass. ptcpl. in -ta,-na 710-13, 786, 802.

Patronymics, formation 828-34; show vrddhi strengthening 834.

Perfect, act. ptcpl. dcln. 348; perfect-system synopsis 447-8; personal endings 448 d, 597-600; of ah- 'to be' 539; perfect-system inflection 592-623; redupl. syllable 592-4; pluperfect 602; modes of the perf. 603-4; pdgm. 605 seq.; periphrastic form 623; perf. pass. ptcpl. 681; perf. desid. 701 N.; act. ptcpl. in -vah 714, 822; mid. ptcpl. in -ana,-ana 715-

Periphrastic, perf. 623; verbal phrases 722-4.

Person in verbal inflections 447.

Personal pronoun 385 seq.; endings of verbs 448; of perf. 497-600.

Pluperfect 602.

Plural, general plur. case 228 seq.

Polysyllables, shorten final long vowels 25-

Possessive pronoun 434-5, 440 N. 3; cpds. 884-6.

Postposition of preposition 736.

Postpositive a in abl. and loc. 222-4, 379-80.

Precative, not quotable 666.

Predicate verb, used only once when prefix repeated 752 N. 2.

Prefixes, advl. 733; nominal 747-8; verbal 749-54; rules for connecting with verb 751; repeated 752; separated from verb 753.

Prepositions, in general 734-7; placed in postpositive position 736.

Prepositional adj. cpds. 889.

Present-system 468-591; causative 687. See Indicative.

Preterite, see pluperfect 602. See Indicative.

Primary, derivation 756-823; treatment of root 757-8.

Proclitics, see Sandhi 898.

Pronominal, dcln. of adjs. 443; derivatives 857 N. 2.

Pronouns, synopsis 377 seq.; personal 385 seq.; relative 399 seq.; interrogative 406 seq.; indefinite 408; demonstrative 409 seq.; possess. 434-5, 440 N. 3; reflexive 435-6.

Pronunciation 6 seq.

Proper diphthongs 54 seq.

Prothesis 69, 71.

Protraction-diphthongs 53.

Punctuation, method in MSS. 5.

Quantity, agreement between Av. and Skt. 15; different from Skt. 16; rules for vowels 23 seq.

Radical syllable, in perfect 595-6; in intensive 704'

Reduction-diphthongs 53; reduction of ya, va to i, u 63; in verbal forms 493-4; of ya to e in compounds 865 N., cf. instr. 239.

Reduplication, general rules 465; redupl. class (third) of verbs 470, 540-53; redupl. syllable of perf. 592-4; absence of redupl. 620; redupl. in aorist 650-2; in desiderative 699-701; in intensive 703; in nouns 745 N. 2; redupl. of orig. s 754 (2).

Reflexive use of personal pronouns 395; reflex, pronoun 435-6.

Relative pronoun 399 seq.

Relationship, nouns of 321, 787.

Repetition of same syllable avoided 194; of pronoun 408; of root in intensive 705; of prefix 752.

CONTENTS.

What the original alphabet was in which the Avesta was written we do not know. The alphabet in which our texts are now preserved bears the stamp of a much later age than the language it presents. The question of the origin of this alphabet in which our MSS. are written has difficulties; but there is little doubt that it is derived from the Pahlavi alphabet of the Sassanian times; it is closely related to the book-Pahlavi. This point must be constantly borne in mind in discussing the letters. The question, moreover, of the transcription of this Avestan alphabet as we now possess it has long been and is still a very vexed one. This is the question, in particular, that forms the chief subject of inquiry in the present paper; but all investigations into the matter of transcription imply a more or less extended study of the alphabet from the standpoint of palaeography, phonetics and philology.

The lack of uniformity in the system of transliterating the Avestan characters is confusing to those pursuing philological studies; it has doubtless also in some degree retarded the advancement of the Avestan cause. From the standpoint of philology, the present necessity of some accordance in the method of transcribing this language is apparent. The time is not far distant, it seems, when scholars should and will tend toward adopting some uniform system. Geldner's new edition of the Avestan texts has practically fixed the number of characters to be transcribed, and should Iranian students now agree—and it is hoped that those in America may perhaps set the example —in adopting some uniform method of transliteration, that shall be practical as well as scientifip, an additional impetus would be given to these studies. Such adoption would be a grateful service to all, particularly to those interested in the linguistic importance of the Avesta to Philology. To write on the subject may not be a thankless task; if some suggestion or hint thrown out lead but a step in the right direction as a guide to others for finding a better way, the labor will be quite repaid. To the linguist, moreover, the comparative table of the various systems of transcription, appended for reference (see Appendix), may not be unacceptable.

In regard to the method of Avestan transliterations, the number of systems is almost legion. Many of them, however, differ from one another only in some minor points; in fact, on most of the ordinary details there is a growing tendency more and more toward uniformity. It is chiefly in a certain few respects—but these points are important ones—that Avestan scholars still mainly disagree. Some of these differences have been due to variations in the Avestan characters of some of the MSS. or to different forms adopted in the editions; but since the new edition has set up a standard, the question of the actual Avestan characters to be transcribed has become practically settled, and it seems as if greater agreement might be brought about. Of course those who have to deal with palaeographic questions of the MSS. will be compelled to add other signs in transliterating, but this need not concern philologists generally. By a few mutual concessions, uniformity and concord in rendering the symbols of the Avestan texts might soon result.

The transcription here offered is presented in a tentative way, in the hope that some of the hints may prove useful for the future. It has been based on personal advice and suggestions upon various points, from names of no less authority—linguistic, palaeographic, philological, and phonetic—than Professors Brugmann, Geldner, Pischel, and Sievers. To these was added weight from the stand- point of epigraphy—

Professor Andreas. Practical suggestions have also been received from Professors Delbriick, Collitz, Hopkins, and Lanman. The marshalling of such names is of itself not without significance; the question is one that really is of interest to many scholars. The opinions on the subject of course varied. The transliteration, which I here suggest, is given as a sort of compromise and concession both to the radical and to the conservative side of the question. The system has endeavored to be at the same time strictly scientific and yet as far as possible practical. With a little good will, perhaps out of this system some uniformity of method might be developed and adopted. In America at least we have now the opportunity of uniting; if a few will take the lead, others will follow.

In preparation of this system the various methods of transliteration (Bartholomae, Hubschmann, Justi, de Harlez, Sacred Books, etc.) have been examined: the aim throughout has been to hold the *mediam viam.*—The main features of the system are (1) that it shall be scientific and at the same time fairly practical. (2) Single characters as far as possible are represented by single signs. This latter is far more practicable, and at the same time more requisite, in Avestan than it is in Sanskrit. (3) It makes concessions as far as possible to existing systems, and as far as may be avoids radical alterations and introductions.— The particular points characterising the system are: (1) a remodelling in transcription of the -vowels;—(2) adoption of the more or less generally used Germanic characters *d, p, j,* for the spirants; similarly also for the nasal, cf. also aspiration;—(3) uniformity in the use of a diacritical sign to differentiate letters. For such a diacritical sign in Avestan, the practical proposal is made to use a subscript tag *t,* (inverted apostrophe, comma, spiritus lenis or the like) to designate the Avestan 'derivation stroke' discussed below p. 16.

In regard to the character of the transliteration as being scientific, it must of course be said that when extensive Avestan printing is to be done

some of the transcription types would have to be cast. But in most offices that do philological work, the majority of the types required are already on hand; the few that may not be, can always be mechanically made without much difficulty. In this way the practical side of the question has been kept in view. In smaller articles the transcription can always be used without the necessity of having the type cast; the signs in general are such as can be made up by any intelligent compositor.1 In this respect the more consistent use of the modifying 'tag' (t t) is very practical. The tag, moreover, when cast on the letter breaks off less easily than the point. For purely popular articles Justi's transliteration somewhat remodelled may of course be retained —see Appendix 'Substitute Alphabet'.

The Av. transcription tentatively proposed is now given. The order of letters is based on that of the Sanskrit alphabet. For convenience of reference, moreover, Justi's transliteration, *Handbuch der Zendsprache,* is given beneath each letter. The letters in parenthesis () show where deviations from Justi have been made.

1 Reference, for example, might here be made to several Notes by the writer in the *American Journal of Philology* 1889—90 where the system was thus employed.

Prdposed Transcription of Avestan.1 (Compared with Justi, *Handbuch der Zendsprache).*

In the above alphabet a certain number of the Avestan characters are simple and have in general corresponding Latin letters that may represent them, All unite now in transcribing these in the ordinary manner. They are— 1 For a merely practical transliteration to be used for popular purposes, see 'Substitute Alphabet' p. 28 below.
2 The signs i, u need be employed only for purely scientific purposes; the letters y, v for both initial and internal TO I) », answer fully for practical purposes. 8 The single sign / is quite sufficient for the three v, g, ro. The differentiation /, /, / need only be made in scientific articles. *a, a, i, i, u, ii, o, d*

*k, g, t, d, p, f, b*
*n, m*
*r*
*s, z, h.*

In regard to the others, questions of greater or less importance arise and there is more or less diversity in respect to them. Beginning with the vowels these may now be taken up in detail.

A. VOWELS.

A Modification in Transcription of the Vowels.

Av. (, j — to, y — K"; C.

3. S— *e, e — a; q. e*-Vowels, l. Av. ( 3 (Justi *e)*. Av. *T±-»h kir3naoiti* (Justi *kerenaoiti)*. The fact that Av. (is not a pure -vowel has long been recognized. There have consequently been various different methods of denoting it, e. g. *Cb* or *a* (Rask, *Ueber d. Alter u. Ec/ itheit der Zend-Sprache)*, *e* (Spiegel, *Av. -Uebersetz.* etc.; Geiger; *Handbuc/i der Awestasprache)*, *e* (Fr. Miiller, *Wiener Zeitschrifi)*, etc. A critical study of this letter shows that it must have represented an obscure sound that seems closely to have resembled the shore indefinite vowel familiar in English, 'gardnr', 'history', 'potato', 'measuring', 'm«tton', 'against', 'forward', 'sachem', 'formidable'. It seems to have approached sometimes more nearly to *a (i)*, sometimes to « *(o).x* A study of the MS. variants in this respect is very instructive.

The rt-tendency of f is seen, for example, in endings e. g. Av.-fory-To *yas-n3m, bar3n* = Skt. *yajhdm, dbharan.*

So GAV. *3Visti* = Skt. *dvitti* Again, observe the interchange between *3* and *a* in the MSS., e. g. *up3m3m* beside *up-a-m3m, mainyavim* beside *mainy-a-vd* etc. Furthermore, the *3* that arises from *a* before *m* or *n* may be palatalized to *i* when either *y, c, j,* or *z* immediately precedes. The variants show the palatal nature of the sound e. g. Av. *4!v"l vacim* beside *4nv-"i vacant* 'voice' = Skt. *vacant*— cf. Jackson, *Avesta Gram.* §§ 29, 30. Independent variants between *3* and *i* occur quite often, even when no palatal precedes, e. g. *n3mata-, nimata-*Vd. 5. 38, *bizaiigra-, b3zatigra-*Ys. 9.18 and many others.

The w-nature beside its /-shading is

also noticeable. In GAV., for example, *3* appears sometimes to be written (as a kind of dissimilation) for *u* or *i*, when in the following syllable an *u (v)* or an *i* stands; the epenthetic vowel may then be also written beside it. This proves the labial character in addition to its palatal. Thus, GAV. _-"»C.j *dr3gvaiit-*'wicked' ( = *drugvan.t*-to Av. *druj-)* GAV. *b3zvatit-* 'advantageous' (= *buzvaiit*-to Skt. *bhuj-*); GAV. *up"rn-*'zeal' (?) Ys. 34.7, cf. *u$-u-ruye* Ys. 32.16; GAV. *hu3Hi-*'well-being' (i.e. *hu;-i-ti-);* GAV. *Sn&ti-*Ys. 30. 11; GAV. *dsk3Hi-*Ys. 44.17. See *Av. Grain.* § 31.

Such interchanges with *a, i, u (0)* are indicative of the intermediate character of the sound.2 For all these reasons, it is here suggested to adopt the transcription *(3)* commonly used in Phonetics (cf. Sweet's *Hist, of Eng. Sounds* 2 ed. p. I 5 etc.) for the sound that seems so closely to resemble it. This choice of the 'turned *e (3)* is a practical one; no new type need be cast. The compositor has simply to reverse the *e (3)*. 1 Cf. Eng. *avowal*, pron. *rvowil*. 2 Palaeographically Av. f is connected with Pahlavi I «, i. e. merely a broken I ((). For some excellent points bearing on the Pahlavi and the Inscriptions in regard to this letter, I am personally indebted to the courtesy of Professor F. C. Andreas.

2. Av. ( S (Justi /). GAV. *fyf" azSm*, ji *n9*, Av.-tnjc (Justi *az/m, nd, gdus)*. The sound *S* is the corresponding long to ( and is therefore to be represented *(i)* in accordance. It is found chiefly in GAV.1 answering to YAV.1 *3, a, d,* 3. Av. *,o e, e* (Justi *e)*. GAV. rwro *yazaite,* YAV. K"f-»yazaite (Justi *yazaite)*.

These two, 10 &, correspond to each other in the MSS., as short and long. They are therefore to be distinguished. Justi etc. in accordance with the first editions gave both as *e*. Later it became customary, as was proper, to distinguish them from one another and a subscript point (thus *e e*) was used to differentiate them from *e e* which were adopted for ( This now is no longer necessary; as we have *3 i* for (, the simple *e e* for 10 may be adopted. That brings them in direct accord with their parallels *0, 0*
4. Av. *m* (Justi *do)*. Av. p3/-"G *mazdd)*

(Justi *tnazdao)*. Palaeographically, *y* is evidently a combination of (*a3.* Phonologically, it seems to have denoted an in 1 GAV. = Gatha Avesta, all that is written in the Gatha dialect.— YAV. = Younger Avesta.

2 Phonetically *i* probably resembled the long drawn English pronunciation of 'word' (waard i. e. *or)*, 'earth.' (aarth i. e. *er)*, 't«rf (taarf i. e. *ur)*, 'f/rst' (faarst i. e. *ir)* etc., cf. Sweet, *Hist, of Eng. Sounds* p. 276. 8 If "t3 are universally rendered *o d*, consistency requires that 10 should likewise be given without the subscript point. Perhaps both sets, however, would orthographically better be given by some diacritical mark e. g. *o, 3, e, i* (though (.) generally denotes a lingual letter). They are not pure sounds. This is shown, for example, by *vohu, cor'(, yesne,* and such MSS. interchanges *e, a, i* etc. It must be remembered that Av. *o, e* — Skt. *d, e* only when final. Ordinarily Skt. *o, e* are represented in Av. by *ao, al*. A fuller discussion must be reserved for some future time. definite -shading of *a*. It fluctuates in the MSS. on the one hand with *a* e. g.-3/" *mazdd* as variant to s/v *mazdd;* on the other hand it is found as a variant for *Y" au* e. g. *rily hratd)* for *y"r-Ay fyratdu*. The palaeographic and phonetic character of the letter, then, are thus given t. (( J) = *m (a a)*.

In printing, *d)* if not provided, may be mechanically made by uniting *a 3* under the macron *a3.* 5. Av. *c q* (Justi *a)*.
Av. *fay ham,* Dc»u£3 *daevqn* (Justi *ham, daevdn)*.

The letter x presents a nasalization of *a, a;* sometimes it also resembles Skt. anusvara. To render it, the character *q* has been preferred to *a*. The symbol *q* is now more generally used in linguistic works to represent the o-sound with nasal coloring. It is preferable in case the question of accenting the vowel (') ever comes up. Of course in popular works *a* may be retained. The symbol *q* may be mechanically made by placing a subscript hook e below the letter.1

B. CONSONANTS.

a. Germanic Letters as Symbols. Spirants.

Av. *b,* t,, *6, t,*

*h J J d*

All scientific work in Avestan implies extensive comparison with Sanskrit; on this account the Av. translitera 1 Strictly the L should be varied somewhat from the 'tag' below referred to, in order to show that it represents a somewhat different modification.

tion is always to be brought into closest symmetry with the Skt. transcription. This is practical and it is necessary. It is necessary, however, on the other hand to avoid confusion with the Sanskrit. Confusion sometimes arises from using a symbol in Av. with a different value from that which it familiarly has in Skt. , or the same sign for sounds that differ enough in Skt. and Av. to require a distinction to be made between them. A striking point, for instance, in which differentiation between the two may be made is in the matter of the Av. spirants. The possession of spirants as contrasted with the Skt. aspirates is one of the characteristic phonetic features of Avestan. For scientific purposes, then, these Av. spirants should be distinguished from the Skt. *kh, gh, th, dh.* Nor is this to be done alone of account of the difference of sound — the symbol having a spirant value in transcribing the one language and an aspirate value in transliterating the other —but also, it might be added, because confusion in Av. may sometimes thus arise from the fact that *gh* in this way should have to stand for the single character *(j)* and for the double letters *arc (gh)* found in G(Y)Av., e. g. GAV. lom-c-. *aojoti-g-h-v-at, f&ti-gh-im,* YAV. *nvr# 'f&m p3sdcitigh.3m.*

To obviate this possibility of confusion, recourse has been had on the one hand to the Gk. characters /, y, 0, X (js) by some (especially Hiibschmann, *Umschreibung der iran. Sprachen;* cf. also *K.Z.* xxiv. p. 323), on the other hand to letters derived from Tuetonic signs *fy, J, p, d* (Rask, Westergaard; esp. Pischel, Bartholomae). The general tendency (e. g. cf. Brugmann, *Grundriss;* etc.) scems now to accept the Germanic rather than the Greek signs; they are therefore here adopted. Comparisons with Greek words, moreover, are more common than with Germanic; less confusion

therefore thus results and such un-Avestan looking words as *yaWd* are likewise avoided. In America, England, and Germany the A. S. *J, d, j* if not actually on hand are always easy to obtain whenever scientific transcription is needed; and $ can be supplied by an Old English or German long *h* (b). Almost all philological typefonts contain the former two, at any rate, of these signs. They possibly are open to some objection from the Romance side; but the substitutions offered under each should be considered. These spirants may now be taken up in detail.

6. Av. *6-//* (Justi *kti*).

Av.-oj1o-"V) *fyratdus* (Justi *khratdus).* Palaeographically the Av. character *6- (kh)* is derived by the upward 'derivation stroke' from the Pahlavi -" *h.* A good transliteration was suggested for it by Pischel *B.B.* vi. p. 275). The character is somewhat similarly derived from the long Gothic *h.* It may always be given by setting an ordinary Old English or German long *h* (b).

7-Av. *vj* (Justi *gh).*

Av.-G *ujram* (Justi *ughreni).* For the spirant the symbol/—the ordinary roughened *g* of the Anglo-Saxon— is used, as often. It is on hand generally in philological type-fonts. If not, it can possibly be given by the long *j* of 05, or better the compositor may set a simple Old English or German *g* (g g g).

8. Av. A *p* (Justi *th).*

Av. *prata* (Justi *thrata).* The dental spirant *6* is derived from the Av. sign for *t* by the upward derivation stroke. It is represented, as often, by the common A. S. 'thorn'; this is certainly found in all type-fonts that do linguistic work.

9. Av. f (Justi *dh).y*

Av. *ida* (Justi *idha).*

The symbol *d* or *db* is the common A. S. 'edh' or crossed *d.2* b. Diacritical Marks on Letters.

In transcribing Oriental alphabets there are always a certain number of characters that may be well represented by merely adding to similar Roman letters a diacritical sign as mark of differentiation. It is proper that the diacritical mark should be used consistent-

ly throughout. Furthermore, since comparisons between Avestan and Sanskrit must constantly be made, it is necessary again to avoid using a diacritically marked letter with a special value in Sanskrit and then employing the same marked letter is a slightly different function in Avestan. Confusion arises from disregard of this point. Thus, Justi's *j* ((») is confusing as it represents a different sound in Av. from that which / (cerebral, lingual) familiarly has in Sanskrit. Again, *h* for Av. % would be confusing on account of Skt. visarga.8

A palaeographic study of the MSS. shows that many of the Avestan characters are actually derived from one another or differentiated by a stroke *t j* or curve which Professor Geldner orally termed a 'derivation stroke'.4 For the voiced labial spirant *w* (Justi *w)*—derived from v by the derivation stroke— the simple letter *w* with the German pronunciation, has been retained as is generally done. A crossed *b* i. e. 2 which is used by some scholars in Gothic transcription, would perhaps well represent it orthographically, but here strict conservatism seems preferable.

1 On I », iS v, V k see below. 8 Scientifically, however, visarga in Skt. seems better transliterated by *h* or the like, the subscript point (.) being reserved for the Unguals *t, (h, d, dh, p.* For many interesting particulars connected with the MSS. in this respect especially, and for valuable hints I am deeply indebted to the kindness of Prof. K. F. Geldner.

Thus c H, to Uj, or or, v & «w, io if,-o gj e':c.—dotted line denoting 'derivation stroke'.1 Systematic treatment suggests that we should adopt some similar method to differentiate the Latin letters whenever it is necessary to designate such modif1cation in transcribing Avestan characters. At the excellent suggestion of Dr. Geldner, a 'tag' (t) has been adopted to be used somewhat in conformity with the 'derivation stroke' whenever it is necessary and possible thus to differentiate. Practical grounds favor such adoption: when the types are cast the 'tag' breaks off less easily; furthermore, it may always be mechanically constructed by an inverted spiritus lenis

( ) set close or even by the turned apostrophe (J. The plan, therefore, is thoroughly practical; the tag will also serve somewhat in recalling the palaeographic character of the letter it is used to designate.2 To prove that the tag as modification can be readily employed, reference may be made to some Avesta Notes by the present writer in the *American Journal of Philology* 1889—90.

The letters diacritically marked by the 'tag' either as sign of differentiation or as a representative of the Av. 'derivation stroke' may now be taken up in detail.

10. Av. £ / (Justi /).

Av. (o-"'Vuj *baraf* (Justi *barat*).

The Av. letter (» is one whose phonetic nature is uncertain. Justi employed *f* to transcribe it. This is open to objection; the subscript point (.) brings in confusion with the Skt. lingual /. Various other devices have been used to represent it—see Appendix p. 31. Whatever the 1 See also Rask, *Echtheit* p. 57, 50, 'Zug', 'Aspiralionszug; Spiegel, *Gram.* p. 17 'durch Anfügung eines Striches'; Hübschmann, *K.Z.* xxiv. p. 339 etc.

a A 'tag' as modification sign is elsewhere in use, cf., for instance, Sweet's *Anglo-Saxon Reader;* Sievers-Cook's *Grammar of Old English,* et al. 2 phonetic value of the letter may have been, its palaeographic character is clear; is formed by the 'derivation stroke' directly from *r t.* It may therefore be consistently represented by *t + (,* thus: is o-+ o = / ? +,;.

Observe that / is mechanically to be made as before by means of the inverted comma shaved off and set close, or by the turned apostrophe.

Nasals.

Av. *is,* i,

, *V, n, ti-*

*ll.* Av. ) » (Justi *n*).

Av. g"m" *avhaf* (Justi *anhaf*).

For the guttural nasal ) (Justi *n*) the symbol *w* derived from the old long tailed Germanic *n* has been adopted. This is the common designation for the guttural nasal in linguistic vtorks.1 In short articles where scientific transliteration is required, the symbol » may be produced mechanically by inverting *a (v)* and

opening the bottom with a penknife, thus *v. 12.* Av.-a *1* (Justi *n*).

Av.-o *daiqhius* (Justi *dainhdus*).

The character-u is palaeographically a modification of i; it occurs for *v* in connection with *h* when preceded by an *i-*or -sound. The two ) / interchange often enough in MS. variants to show the resemblance that-a must have had to % in form and in force. The palaeographic cha 1 The sign *A* (Justi) should be reserved for the Skt. palatal *A* (Whitney fl)—see the suggestion by Pischel, *Gott. gel. Anz.,* 14. Juni 1882, p. 738 seq. The letter » is preferable also for the guttural nasal in Skt. (Whitney «) when comparisons with Av. are made.

racter of-a, the transcription consistently recognizes by attaching the modification tag (£) to *w,* thus forming 13. Av. £! *ft* (Justi *n*).

Av. !o,pA3 *baratiti* (Justi *barenti*). Palaeographically # is composite character representing an a-sound with *n.* In appearance it resembles «. 4 of the MSS. In usage, however, # is merely a modification of 1 *n* before stopped consonants. According to the system, therefore, it will be represented by *n* with the modification tag. This tagged *n (tQ* recalls on the one hand the true w-character of on the other its external resemblance to the nasalized . *q.* Sibilants.

Av. »,-o, gj, ro — no.

*s, S, S, S — z* 14. Av. u *s* (Justi f).

Av. *riy asti, 'vo" aspd* (Justi *afti, acpo*). The letter u shares the nature both of the palatal and of the dental sibilant. It is now universally given by *s;* this is therefore adopted.2 15. Av. (s, ro) *s ($, $),* Justi *s (sh, sk).* Av.-oio *ratus, una' is' us,* i4"«ro *§yaojna* (Justi *ratus, ishus, skyaothna*).

From a palaeographic standpoint it is evident at a glance that-o forms the basis of the three j-sounds. The sign *s* must therefore likewise form the basis of the three transliterations. It is customary thus to transcribe-o by *s* rather than by *s,* in. order to avoid confusion with the Skt.

1 Justi's « is open to the objection that scientifically the acute () should be reserved for designating accent. 8 For the palatal -s.in Skt. (Whitney f) it seems

preferable to use *i* when comparisons between Av. and Skt. are to be made. lingual $ noted above. Justi's *s* for o has had of course to be abandoned. Now since is a composite character made by the derivation stroke, it may be consistently rendered by use of the modification tag, thus

M (L-+-o) = / *(e + s*).

In like manner ro is palaeographically a modification of-o before *y.* This differentiation by means of the ) turned in the other direction may be indicated by the reversed tag *§.*

The threefold differentiation of *s, £* is not necessary except in transcribing a text for scientific purposes where it is desired to reproduce the differences of the original. For practical purposes, the sharp distinction may be quite disregarded;-o is final (except before *t, c*), initial and internal, ro only before ». The simple *s* will therefore practically suffice i. e.

-*v s* t& *f* or all simply *s.*

ro

The sign i is on hand in all linguistic type-fonts. The differentiation if found necessary, may of course easily be made as before by means of the subscript tag.1 This concludes the sibilants. 2

Aspiration.

-A-v *v,* i".

*h, fy, k*

The fundamental aspirate is & *h* (Justi *h*). It is a modification of the Pahlavi *h.* In the transliteration of it, all are agreed. In regard to the other two *r* there is a diversity in treatment. Justi wrote both as *q;* but they 1 The ligature «0 St, Kjo *lc* require no further special designation. The voiced spirant sibilant JO (Justi *zl,*) is commonly rendered *i* in conformity with /. No remark is needed.

are sharply to be distinguished. They will be examined in detail. 16. Av. £ *k* (Justi *q*).

Av. h»e£3 *dahjunqm* (Justi *daqyunani*). The character is a mere modification of *h* (Pahlavi before a *y.* It may be thus represented:

G (U +-) = *h 0 + h*).

The *h-sign* (Pahlavi is the basis; the 'derivation stroke is represented by the 'tag'.

17. Av. *v hr* (Justi *q*). Av. -"*v ha*-(Justi *qa*-).

The letter c is a ligature of Pahlavi-" *h* and 1 *z/*. It interchanges at times with »or *hv*. To transcribe this ligature, the suggestion is here made that we may aptly use *h*, in itself a similar ligature, that is often used in' Gothic translitera-tion, e. g. Braune's *Goth. Gram*, transl. by Balg, 1883, cf. § 63. Thus: i" (1-") = *hr (h v)*.

As this sign is not always on hand, its place may be supplied by *h* with a slightly raised *v*, thus *k"*.

Semivowels. Av. *ro (") y* (Justi *y*), 1 (») *v* (Justi *v*). Av. wmioTO *yesnyo, fr vtdva* (Justi *yecnyo, vidhvad*).

The characters ro *If*, as is familiarly known, occur when initial; the forms *»* are found when internal. The simple transcription *y, v* for both the initial and the internal forms has been retained on conservative grounds. The same are re-tained likewise by Brugmann, *Grun-driss der indogerm. Sprachen*. Confu-sion can hardly arise; the exceptions to the law of the initial-internal forms need scarcely be noticed. Scientifically, how-ever, it is more accurate to adopt *i u* for *» »* as has been done by others. Thus: w *y* I . I or both simply *y. b v* or both sim-ply *v*.

*» I*

Palatals. Av. *v c* (Justi *c*),. R *j* (Justi *j*). Av. 4ivW *cipram, »-"vjasaiti* (Justi *cithretn, jagaiti*).

The voiced palatal is palaeographi-cally a derivative from *v*. In transcribing *Y %* it seems best to be conservative; Justi's *c, j* are retained; they are like-wise kept by Brugmann, *Grundriss*. The same is almost universally the case in transcribing Sanskrit. Those who wish to be more scientific in this respect are welcome of course to the palatal point over *k, g*, thus *k, g*.

Resume.

Such in the main are the characteris-tics, palaeographic and phonetic, of the letters in the Avestan alphabet upon which there is most discussion; such likewise is the system of transliteration proposed. I have adopted it for my Avesta Series.; i. Grammar, ii. Texts,

shortly to appear. Many of the points in regard to the alphabet are, to be sure, more or less familiar; in such cases the transcription adopted has merely fol-lowed what it seems the general tenden-cy to adopt. May these points become more and more universally agreed up-on! The new points in the transliteration are suggestions toward uniformity or to-ward improvement by remodelling. On the latter, compare for instance the dis-cussion of the -vowels.

The principal features of the tran-scription suggested may now, therefore, be recalled. They are the consistent use of the 'tag' as a diacritical mark, instead of points or accents. This 'tag', let it be remembered, answers in general to the 'derivation stroke' by which palaeo-graphically so many of the Av. char-acters are formed or modified. Further-more, the system marks, clearly the or-thographic distinction of the three s i b i l a n t s *s, $, g*, when necessary, also of the nasals *», ff, n, ti*, and of the aspirate *h, , hr*. A practical transcription of the much-discussed *£* / (Justi *f*) is suggest-ed. An innovation is made by remodel-ling the *e*-vowels, using *3,3* as an apt representation of the uncertain ( , and thus bringing w *e* "s» *o 5* into closer re-lationship — however the latter be ren-dered. With reference to *f c, J*, ou *w*, ro *» y*, ) *» v*, conservativism has been used. The Germanic characters *J, d*, etc. have been adopted for the spirants according to what seems to be the apparent ten-dency of the present.

In conclusion I would like once more to renew my cordial thanks to each of the scholars mentioned at the beginning of the paper. Their courtesy, their sug-gestions and their advice are cordially appreciated. To Professor Geldner, as always, is my gratitude due for the in-terest that he personally took in dis-cussing the various sides of the question of Avestan sounds and of their tran-scription, as well as for the trouble he went to, not alone in giving me valuable points in regard to palaeography, but al-so for making accurate copies of many letters and styles of MS. writing. To these obligations may be added my in-debtedness to the publisher, Herrn W.

Kohlhammer, and to the compositor, Herrn Sauberlich, for the form and for the accuracy with which the paper is presented.

It remains alone to repeat the hope that Avestan scholars may strive more toward union in transliteration. The above system represents in most points what seems to be the general drift in regard to scientific transcription of the Avesta; it has only added or modified where alterations seemed necessary; and the practical side of the question, withal, has been kept as much as possi-ble in view. If its main points should re-ceive the sanction only of certain schol-ars, how many there would be would follow these!

July 1890.

A. V. Williams Jackson Columbia College
New York City.

Appendices. Appendix I.

Proposed Transcription of Avestan. (Compared with Justi, *Handbuch der Zendsprache*).1 2 The signs *i, u* need only be employed for purely scientific purposes; the letters *y, v* for both initial and internal TO , *If »*, answer fully for practical purposes. 8 The differentiation /, /, / need only be made in scientific articals. The single sign *l* is ordinarily quite sufficient for the three "O, ft, ro. Appendix II.

Suggestions to the Printer.

For small articles when special types not cast.

(See Alphabet, Appendix I.)

Vowels *3, 3, m*.

The *3* is simply a 'turned' *e. — i*, turned *3* with macron (-) as quantity mark.—For *a*, set *a 3* close together by shaving edge of type a little; then unite under macron.

Unusual Signs *fy, j, J, d, w, h-*.

For *fy, j*, set Old English or German or similar long *h, g.—p, dare* Anglo-Saxon 'thorn', 'edh'.—, inverts *(v)* open and shape with penknife *v*, or set differ-ent *n.—h*, substitute *h*.

Tagged Letters /, *tj, ti, fy, q*.

Use a turned spiritus lenis, or set in-verted apostrophe. —*q*, differentiate tag somewhat, i f desired.

Optional Letters *§, i, u*.

Presumably, *s* is on hand. For /, /, if needed in purely scientific articles, set tag and cedilla beneath *s*.— For *i, u,* if likewise needed, shave off *n* and set close beneath.

Appendix III.

Substitute Alphabet.-

For popular articles.

(Modelled after Justi.)

A. Vowels.

Short *a i u 3 o*

Long *a i ii i o (5 q* or *d*

B. Consonants. Guttural *k kh g gh*

Palatal *c — j —*

Dental *t th d dh /*

Labial *p f b W*

Nasal *w* or *n %* or *ri n ti* or *n m*

Semivowel and Liquid *y r V*

Sibilant *s i* or *2 z* or *zh*

Aspirate *h fy*

Ligature *fa* or *q* 1 For suggestions to the Printer see Appendix II.

Appendix IV.

Some of the different Systems of Transcription.

(References to the following Works — see Bibliography below.)

Anquetil Du Perron—*Zend Avesta* (1771)—Vol. ii. p. 424. Rask—*Alter u. Echtheit d. Zendsprache,* iibersetz. Hagen (1826) pp. 46, 81. Burnouf—*Le Yacna* (1833) p. xxxvii seq. Spiegel—(Works) e.g. *Av. iibers.* (1852—63); *Commentar* (1864—8); *Vergl. Gram.* (1882). *YikVG-Gathas* (1858—60); *Essays* (1862—84); *Zd. Pahl. Gloss.* (1867). Lepsius— *Das urspriingliche Zendalphabet* (1862). Justi—*Handbuch der Zendsprache* (1864). Roth—(Contributions) e. g. *Kalender* (Z.D.M.G. xxiv); *Bet trdge* (Z.D.M.G. xxv); *Yacna 31* (1876). Fr. Muller—*Zendstudien* iv (Wien. Ac. Mai 1877); *Beitrdge u. Mittheilungen* (Wiener Zeitschrift 1887 seq.). Hubschmann—*Iran. Studien* (K. Z. xxiv. p. 370.—1877—9); *Umschreibung* (1882). Pischel—*Umschreibung* (B.B. vi. p. 272.—1881); *Recension* (Gott. gel. Anz. 1882 p. 737). De Harlez—*Manuel de la langue de I'Avesta* (1882). Sacred Books Of The East—*Translit. of Oriental Alph.* Geldner—*Metrik 187 7); Studien(1882); DreiYasht(1884);* (later contributions) in *K.Z.* and *B.B.* Bartholomae—*Verbum*

(1878); *Gathas* (1879); *Ar. Forsch.* i. (1882); *Handbuch* (1883); *A. F.* ii—iii. (1886—7), and (later contributions) in *K.Z.* and *B.B.* Brugmann—*Grundriss der vergl. Gram.* (1886—English transl. 1888).

Appendix V.

Partial Bibliography.

Writings on the Avestan Alphabet and its Transcription.

Anquetil Du Perron—*Zend-Avesta, Ouvrage de Zoroastre,* ii. p. 425.—Paris 1771. R. Rask—*Ueber das Alter icnd Echtheit der Zend-Sprache,* iibersetzt von F. H. v. d. Hagen, pp. 46—81.—Berlin 1826.

E. Burnouf—*Commentaire stir le Yacna;* L'Alphabet Zend, pp. xxxii—cliii.—Paris 1833. H. Brockhatjs—*Vendidad Sade,* p. xii. Alphabet.—Leipzig 1850.

— in *Zeitschrift der deutschen morgenlandischen Gesellschaft,* xvii. p. 539.

C. Arendt—*Phonetisc/ie Bemerkungen* (Kuhn's Beitrage ii. p. 429).— 1861. M. Haug—*Essays on the Parsis* (1 ed. p. 52—57; 3 ed. West, p. x).—Bombay, London 1862 — 1884.

— *Zand-Pahlavi Glossary* p. 81. Alphabet.—Bombay, London 1867.

Lepsius—*Das urspriinglic/ie Zendalphabet* (in philolog. u. histor. Abhandlungen d. kgl. Ak. der Wissenschaften zu Berl. 31. Marz u. 14. Juli 1862).—Berlin 1863.

F. Justi—*Handbuch der Zendsprache* p. x seq.—Leipzig 1864. Fr. Spiegel—*Gratntn. der altbaktr. Spr ache.—*Leipzig 1867.

— *Vergleichende Gratntn. der altdranischen Sprachen.—* Leipzig 1882.

— *Zur Gesckichte des Avesta Alphabets* (Bezzenberger's Beitrage, ix. p. 173).—1885.

Kuhn & Schleicher—*Umschreibiing des altindischen und altbaktrischen Alphabets* (Kuhn u. Schleicher's Beitrage z. vergl. Sprachforschung v. p. 144).—1868.

Fr. Muller—*Zendstudien* iv: Ueber die Zischlaute des Altbacktrischen. (Sitzb. d. k. Akademie d. Wissensch. — Mai 1877.)—Wien 1877.

H. Hubschmann—*Iranische Studien* i: Ueber den lautwerth des Zendalphabet.—Mit 3 Tafeln. (Kuhn's Zeitschrift xxiv. p. 323—427.)—Berlin 1878—9.

— *Die Umschreibung der iranischen Sprachen und des Armenischen.—*Leipzig 1882.

C. Salemann—*Ueber eine Parsenharidschrift der kaiserl. offentl. Bibliothek zu St. Petersburg.—*Leyden 1879. Could not consult.

C. De Harlez—*De VAlphabet avestique et de sa Transcription.—*Paris 1880. Could not consult.

— *De la Transcription de TAlphabet avestique* (Bezzenberger's Beitrage vii. pp. 127—139).—1883.

Sacred Books Of The East—*Transliteration of Oriental Alphabets* (see end of each volume).—London 1880 seq.

R. Pischel—*Die Umschreibung des Baktrischen* (Bezzenberger's Beitrage iv. pp. 272—282).—Gottingen 1881.

— *Recension von Bartholomae's 'Arischen Forschungen* i' (Gotting. gel. Anz. 14. Juni 1882 p. 737 seq.).

Kirste—*Die constitutionellen Verschiedenheiten der Verschlusslaute im Indogermanischen* p. 7 seq.—Graz 1881. Could not consult.

K. F. Geldner—*Metrik des jiingeren Avesta* p. xiv. Mere mention.—Tubingen 1877.

— *Studien zum Avesta* i. p. 4. Mere mention.—Strassburg 1882.

— *Miscellen aus dem Avesta.* On *e,* «. (Kuhn's Zeitschrift xxvii. p. 257 seq.)—1883.

— *Drei Yasht aus dem Zendavesta* pp. vi—xv. On the sibilants.—Stuttgart 1884.

Chr. Bartholomae—*Das altiranische Verbum* p. ii. Alphabet.—Munchen 1878.

— *Die Gdthds:* Metrum, Text u. s. w. p. 3.—Halle 1879.

— *Arische Forschungen* i: Anhang pp. 155—163.—Halle 1879.

— *Ar. Forsch.* ii—Hi Vonvort.—Halle 1886—.

— *Beitrdge zur altiranischen Grammatik* i. On sibilants and nasals. (Bezzenberger'sBeitriigevii. pp. 188—195.)-1883.

— *Handbuch der altiranischen*

*Dialekte.*—Leipzig 1883. E. Dillon—*Die Umschreibung der eranischen Sprachen* pp. 1—16.—Leipzig 1883. D. Peshotan Sanjana—*Civilization of the Eastern Iranians*

Vol. ii. pp. 273—286 (The Iranian Alphabets, transl. from Spiegel's Eranische Alterthumskunde iii. pp. 759—771).—London 1886. P. De Lagarde—*Mittheilungen* ii. Bemerkungen liber die Awesta-Schrift pp. 38—48.—Gottingen 1887. K. Brugmann—*Grundriss der vergleichenden Grammatik der indogerm. Sprachen* Bd. i. p. vii, 25; Bd. ii. Vor wort pp. vii—viii.—Strassburg 1886—1889.—English translation 1888.